What people are saying about

Is This a Dream?

In *Is This a Dream?*, Dr. Kumar gradually and skillfully reveals who we are, what we are, and how we relate to the world. Dr. Kumar has studied Advaita Vedanta since childhood and is uniquely placed to merge the fields of science, philosophy, and spirituality. This book is a concise, no jargon spiritual handbook. Clarity and wisdom from Dr. Kumar's personal journey convey gems of ancient wisdom in a contemporary context. Read this book and save yourself what could be years of figuring out the answers to life's biggest questions.
Jac O'Keeffe, Spiritual teacher, Author, APST founder

T0163019

Is This a Dream?

Reflections on the Awakening Mind

Is This a Dream?

Reflections on the Awakening Mind

Anoop Kumar

Foreword by Deepak Chopra, MD

MANTRA
BOOKS

Winchester, UK
Washington, USA

JOHN HUNT PUBLISHING

First published by Mantra Books, 2019
Mantra Books is an imprint of John Hunt Publishing Ltd., No. 3 East Street,
Alresford, Hampshire SO24 9EE, UK
office@jhpbooks.com
www.johnhuntpublishing.com
www.mantra-books.net

For distributor details and how to order please visit the 'Ordering' section on our website.

Text copyright: Anoop Kumar 2018

ISBN: 978 1 78904 251 1
978 1 78904 252 8 (ebook)
Library of Congress Control Number: 2018960410

A CIP catalogue record for this book is available from the British Library.

Design: Stuart Davies

UK: Printed and bound by CPI Group (UK) Ltd, Croydon, CR0 4YY
US: Printed and bound by Thomson-Shore, 7300 West Joy Road, Dexter, MI 48130

We operate a distinctive and ethical publishing philosophy in
all areas of our business, from our global network of authors to
production and worldwide distribution.

Contents

To all those who gaze beyond the horizon with feet on the ground.

Foreword by Deepak Chopra

It's a rare book that distills a lifetime of insights and offers them to enlighten others. This book does both. Anoop Kumar immediately struck a chord when we met some years ago. Our medical training was an obvious link, but Anoop struck me as far more than a caring physician, although he is certainly that.

More than anyone I've met, Anoop pays attention to every aspect of waking up, which I'd define as the process of expanding one's awareness and seeing through all old conditioning, habits, and self-defeating beliefs. When you are fully awake, you are whole. At the same time, the world around you becomes whole. As I remember it, my first conversation with Anoop was about the nature of the world, with little preliminary introduction. Many conversations followed, inspired by his obvious delight in uncovering spiritual truths.

More than that, Anoop has delved into consciousness from top to bottom. This is critical to the contents of this book, because leading a conscious life has become more and more important to modern people. We are waking up to the possibility of our unlimited potential. For this to become real, each person must stop leading an unconscious life. Every day we are faced with choices that could expand our awareness, and once begun, this expansion never ends. By the same token, we are offered choices that could contract our awareness, leading to insecurity, self-doubt, and anxiety.

The unconscious life causes pain and suffering by keeping us stuck in a contracted state. The symptoms aren't hidden. The multi-billion-dollar market for antidepressants and tranquilizers keeps expanding. Opioid addiction has reached crisis proportions. Days and nights spent playing video games and surfing the Internet speak to how desperately people seek distractions from facing what their lives really are.

1

Reality isn't "out there" but "in here" — it is always personal. Therefore, the most healing thing you can do is to wake up. In other words, you undertake the journey of self-discovery, with the goal of becoming more conscious. What we aren't aware of, we cannot change. Anoop offers a path to healing by making the reader more aware, and as the process of waking up unfolds, the body and mind find their own resources for returning to a state of balanced well-being.

From the beginning, I was struck by the fact that this young man led two lives, as a practicing emergency physician and a seeker of wisdom. Anoop would agree with me, I hope, that all of us are leading double lives even if we don't realize it. Our outer occupation in the so-called real world is paralleled by an inner life. Contrary to social expectations, it's the inner life that determines a person's ability to grow and evolve. To be human is to belong to a species of consciousness as much as a species of higher primate — we are the only creatures on earth who can consciously transcend our physical limitations. This much is obvious: we fly without wings, we inhabit the most inhospitable climates, and we bend Nature to our will.

But can we transcend our own divided nature, which is at once peaceful and violent, loving and fearful, creative and destructive? Anoop has explored these issues with remarkable insight and subtlety. In Part I he takes on the central topic of identity, presenting his unique take on the question of who we are. In Part II he shifts his attention to the world itself, taking the reader on a journey that weaves together our two lives, out there and in here.

Along the way, he pauses to address common misconceptions about consciousness, especially the notion that the physical interactions of atoms and molecules in the brain are responsible for creating the mind. I'm impressed that Anoop's argument doesn't simply reject neuroscience, which after all has entered a golden age for understanding the brain. His vision is of science as compatible with our subjective awareness. This book is a deep exploration of higher consciousness, but it remains grounded in everyday experiences that anyone can relate to.

In Part III we get a vision of wholeness, the state of unity consciousness when the divided self has been fully healed. Updating the ancient teachings of Vedanta from India, Anoop bases his vision on the fact that there is only one reality, not a different reality for body and mind. Communicating how wholeness can be lived isn't easy, but for me, Anoop has gotten there. In the end, that's what makes his book a must-read for anyone fascinated by life's spiritual possibilities—possibilities that only open up through self-discovery.

Acknowledgements

Thank you, Malini, Surya, Anjali, Mom, Dad, and the many teachers of the Chinmaya Mission.

Thank you to the thousands of patients I've had the honor of serving in the emergency department over the years. You've shown me that life has no separate compartments.

Thank you, Deepak. Through our friendship over the last few years, I've had the chance to participate in conversations with brilliant and diverse minds around the world. I've found that when all is said and done, all minds ask the same big questions and gravitate toward the same big answer.

Introduction

Wonder surrounds us. It's there in the sun hanging in the sky and in the moon coolly illumining the ground at night. It's also here, in the environment around you now. The walls. The furniture. Your clothes. There was a time when even these ordinary, inconspicuous things were wondrous experiences. Remember? It was decades ago, when you had just emerged as a part of this world.

Later, you were taught to replace that wondrous experience with a label—like "wall"—and in doing so, an experience became a thing. Soon, the wonder was forgotten, except for those rare moments when faced with an experience so profound that it shuts down the labeling mechanism—perhaps when reuniting with a loved one or gazing at the speckled night sky.

Must we reduce an experience to the measurements we have tailored? Or, must we ignore our ability to measure so that we may live in Wonderland? Do we have to choose?

I vote no. We can play with both.

The choice I just presented is a false one. It's false in the sense that these two poles—subjective and objective experience—are no different than last year's winter, which came and went. In the midst of that winter, the cold was real, as the many snowmen in our neighborhoods attested. But a few months later, the snowmen had disappeared, and along with them, another winter.

The same happens with all dichotomies, whether they be subjective and objective, cold and hot, me and you, or even our favorite—good and evil. All of these are perspectives that come and go. They are not the final word. That's not to diminish their significance. They are indeed necessary to live as a human being in this world. At the same time, they are also polarized expressions of something more fundamental—life prior to the refracting lens, where there are no dichotomies of any kind.

I wrote this book because a hypothesis I mulled over many years ago kept coming up in my mind. This was the hypothesis: *There are no true contradictions—only apparent ones.* The full import of those words wasn't clear to me, but they sent me on a journey of reconciling everything I experienced with everything I already knew, whether it was in the form of science, philosophy, religion, relationships, or simply taking out the trash and cutting the lawn. I found that reconciling these disparate perspectives required an examination. That journey of reconciling the many compartments of life was crystallized in reflections written over the last couple of years. This book brings those reflections together in one place, assembled in an order that is easy to navigate.

The journey starts with a jolt in Part I by declaring outright, "You're not who you think you are." Thus begins an exploration of identity—the core factor that is at the heart of not only spirituality, but also science, philosophy, religion, and every other facet of life, including washing the dishes on Saturday night after the guests leave.

In Part II, we shift our gaze to the world around us. What is it after all? How does it relate to who I am and how I experience the world? As we explore these questions, the falseness of the dichotomy of you and the world around you is exposed.

In Part III, we take a closer look at the philosophy of non-duality, which is the framework I use throughout the book. I chose to add this analysis to the book for two reasons. First, it gives you a backstage pass to my own thinking and biases. Second, non-duality is making a comeback.

Non-duality was originally expounded several millennia ago in the Indian philosophy of Advaita Vedanta, which translates to "non-dual culmination of knowledge." Today, if you google "non-duality," you will be greeted by a variety of conferences, discussions, and spiritual teachers that are interpreting the same timeless knowledge in a modern context. The inevitable result is that there are varying perspectives on exactly what non-duality means and what its implications are.

Into this sea of voices, I add my own in an attempt to put the sea itself in perspective. Importantly, I present these views on non-duality as someone who is drawing a map of the terrain, not as a scholar of Advaita Vedanta. The purpose of Part III is to put varying perspectives in context, not declare verbatim what has already been said or pit one interpretation against another.

At every step of the way, I urge you to challenge the words you read. They are not meant to convince you, but rather to stimulate reflection. Pick the words up off the page, take them apart, look at them every which way, and see if you can discern the fruit of your own meaning amidst the husk. That is where we meet. There is no discovery in believing or disbelieving what I say.

We are now upon a time in which our perspectives on spirituality, science, philosophy, and religion have evolved enough to stand together in the glare of the spotlight as we ask the most practical of questions:

What is the common truth among all these?
How does it change my life right now?
How does it change the world?

Any answer that doesn't address all these questions is incomplete. Any perspective that rejects another without assimilating it is outdated.

What we are looking for is a complete, comprehensive, living answer—an answer that transforms.

It starts with inquiring into this character called *i*.

Part I

You're Not Who You Think You Are

Chapter 1

Missing Person

"You're not who you think you are," the detective said. His warm eyes and lush eyebrows made him seem more friend than stranger.

Maggie rolled her eyes. "I do know who I am. I'm Maggie." She paused for a moment. "Are you saying I was kidnapped? That there's some period of my life I can't remember?"

"I wouldn't put it quite that way, but you're not that far off," came the reply.

"Friendly or not, this guy is full of it," Maggie thought to herself as she traced a circle on the floor with her toe. "He says just enough to keep me listening, but he's vague enough to be useless. I knew I shouldn't have hired him."

When she had stepped into the detective's office twenty minutes ago, she was hopeful that he would be the right person to help her. She'd tried everything else already: talking to her closest friend, reading a ton of self-help books, confiding in her guidance counselor at school, and, at the urging of her parents, even seeing a psychiatrist. But three years and four prescription medications later... nada. Nobody seemed to understand what she was trying to say.

Hiring a missing-persons detective was admittedly a stretch, but Maggie figured that it just may take a wild idea to solve an unusual problem: she couldn't figure out why she felt like she was episodically disappearing during the day. It was like she didn't know who she was, or even if she was. Hiring a detective to help find herself was unusual, but she felt her only other option was to join her friends on the weekend and drink herself into oblivion. "Not such a bad idea considering how this is going," she thought.

Maggie waited for the detective to elaborate on his reply. What did he mean by, "You're not that far off"? He had been vague, so it was his responsibility to clarify. Besides, she didn't want to appear too eager. "It's not like I'm completely confused or anything," she reassured herself. "So what if he doesn't figure it out?" A wisp of fear arose in her.

The detective said nothing and shifted in his old wooden chair, eliciting a creak that resounded through the large room. The air was thick and warm and hung over them like a drape.

"What do you mean I'm not who I think I am?" she finally asked.

"Your parents gave you the name Maggie when you were born right?" He didn't wait for an answer. "So, who were you before you developed the personality of Maggie?"

Her mind was searching.

The detective went on, "You were alive for nine months in your mother's womb. And you may have been in this world for hours or more after your birth without a name, which according to you is your identity. Who were you then, before you were Maggie?" The chair creaked again, punctuating his question.

"I... was a baby." She spoke without finding meaning in her words.

He didn't relent. "You didn't know you were a baby then. You learned to call yourself a baby. Try this. What was your experience then?"

Maggie grew frustrated. "How do you expect me to remember what it was like to be baby?!" She glared at him.

The detective was unfazed. He'd seen the frustration before and he'd surely see it again. Frustration and anger were common reactions at this stage.

"You don't have to remember," he explained. "You just have to see that your personality—what you call Maggie—is an overlay on top of what you are, what you've always been."

Maggie wanted to ridicule his strange theory. It was

preposterous! She wanted to stay angry and prove the detective wrong. But she couldn't. She was tired of fighting. His words rippled across her mind.

The detective continued. "Maggie arrives every time you wake up in the morning. And she leaves when you go to sleep. In fact, she comes and goes all day long. Most people don't notice that because they are their name. They are their personality. The reason you reported yourself missing is because you're starting to wake up from Maggie."

The room was quiet.

Q&A

1. *If my personality is an overlay, what is it overlaid upon?*

The personality that is reading this is one aspect of you. Perhaps we can call that your personal mind. Just as this personal mind is something you are experiencing now, you can also experience deeper layers of yourself, beyond the personality. The deeper you go, the less the experience is unique to you as an individual. A common metaphor that is used is that of waves in the ocean. A wave, deep down, is the ocean whose water doesn't distinguish one wave from the other. Similarly, the deeper layers of "you" beyond the personality are not unique to the individual you. Those layers can collectively be called the mind, appearing as the forms, bodies, and personalities of the world.

2. *Sometimes when I drive, I don't realize that I'm driving. I just kind of end up at a destination but don't remember the actual process of getting there. Is that related to what was happening with Maggie?*

Yes. You and I as individuals are the dance of the outer layer of the mind. We have become so identified with this outer aspect of ourselves that we believe that if this outer layer goes away, what we are would disappear. In fact, everyone has experienced the opposite. We often lose awareness of ourselves as bodies and personalities, only to regain that awareness later. It may be a matter of seconds, hours, days, or longer. In the interval, we don't cease to exist—we simply experience life differently. When the old sense of identity returns and recognizes its recent absence, it often wonders, "Where did I go?"

3. *In the story, the detective asks Maggie who she was before she was Maggie. Are you talking about past lives?*

The detective is simply pointing to the fact that there is a state of being that is prior to the personality, prior to the personal, localized sense of identity. Past lives are with regard to your body and your personal mind—the forms that represent you. What you are at the deepest levels is not a form, not a thing. That deeper You is prior to the birth and death of form. Our birthdates are the dates the forms we are wearing now came into being, and one day these forms will again trans-form.

Chapter 2

Love, Shining!

Love is at the root of what we are. When children are born, they are soaked in love. This is why we adore babies. Love radiates from their every glance, every movement. They remind us of what lies within.

As children grow up, they begin to accumulate beliefs from others, often from those who no longer feel the love radiating within. The beliefs pile up. And they seem to snuff out the love. The children begin to feel lonely, disconnected, separate.

And they wonder, *where is the love?*

And so, they search. They search in friends and family. They search in spirituality and science. They search in books and poems. They search in drugs and alcohol. They search in food and sex. And for a while some of these seem to work.

And now the children have grown into adults. But they haven't dis-covered love. It's still covered up by those beliefs.

One day the beliefs become too much to bear. It becomes obvious that the lessons aren't working. Through frustration, insight, and perhaps a sprinkle of good fortune, the weary adults begin to shed their beliefs, one by one. They dare to stand naked again. And the love that was always there floods them once more.

There is only one love, and that is the love that radiates within. It is at the root of every human being. When you feel that you are receiving love from someone or something, look closely, and you will recognize that it is your own love that has been unleashed, gushing forth from within and enveloping you.

There is no prerequisite for love. Nobody has to give you love. Nobody has to validate you. Love is within you in infinite supply right now. If you do not feel this, check the mind for any accumulated beliefs that are dimming its expression—beliefs about who you are, who you should be, and how you should act. One by one, strike them out and weed them out of your life. One way to help make this exercise concrete is by writing all those beliefs down, reviewing them one by one, recognizing what role each is playing in your life, and drawing a line through the ones that don't serve you anymore.

The more the beliefs are weeded out, the more the love that is already within you shines.

Q&A

1. *What do you mean when you say there is only one love?*

In the previous chapter, I suggested that our bodies and personalities are only the outer layer of what we are. As we go deeper into our nature, we find that things that appear to be separate and distinct on the outside, such as people and things, are in fact immersed in a sea of awareness. You can replace the word *awareness* with whatever you'd like: consciousness, knowing, presence, or simply make up a word. It doesn't matter. The point is there is an experience that is beyond separation. When that *knowing* (as I'll call it now) comes into contact with our bodies, personalities, or any other thing, there is the recognition of non-separation, which is experienced as love.

This one love filters through the mind and is experienced as the many forms of conditional love we see in the world.

2. *What about the love I feel from my spouse? Does that also come from me?*

All love that you experience comes from within you, without exception. When someone accepts us as we are, we drop our self-judgements, and in that moment, the love that was always there is experienced. It was our own self-judgements and misconceptions that were blinding us to the love to begin with. If the self-judgements are then not taken up again, the feeling of love will persist, whether or not a loved one is present.

This doesn't mean we can't develop personal affection. We surely can. It's just that personal affection, no matter how enjoyable, can't outshine the underlying love that connects us all.

3. *Is experiencing that love the purpose of life?*

Experiencing that love changes the way we experience life. We might say that it changes our way of being. In that sense, it's often said that recognizing this love is the purpose of life. Such a goal may help the individual stay oriented toward something as they investigate their own experience.

4. *Is love our ultimate nature?*

What we are is boundless. We may say that it experiences itself through us. Its many expressions go by many names depending on their quality—love, joy, ecstasy, bliss, and so on. It also includes feelings that are generally considered negative, such as sadness and anger. Ultimately, these are aspects or grades of that which is beyond description. Even words such as *boundless* and *infinite*, though often used, do not really tell us what we are. They only negate what we are not.

Chapter 3

What Is the Ego?

The ego is the aspect of the mind that feels personal. It emanates the boundary of "me" and "I." We can observe in a newborn child that the personal sense of "me" has not yet crystallized. A newborn may be crying loudly one moment and perfectly content the next. States of mind seem to come and go without a central identity holding on to experiences.

By the age of two, toddlers start to use words like "me." "Mine" can become a favorite word in this stage. This is a sign of the ego crystallizing. The greater mind is creating a demarcation within itself, a sub-identity, which we have given a first and last name.

On close inspection, we see that this sub-identity is not a thing in itself, but rather a bundle of thoughts infused with energy. For example, the thought "name Joe" may have been repeated thousands of times by the age of two. That thought will have occurred in association with many experiences of happiness and unhappiness, creating a close association of thoughts, including "name Joe," "mine," "me," and "I." If these thoughts occurred only once in a while, they might be like any other thoughts that come and go. But their close proximity is what causes them to interrelate strongly, which creates the experience of a new sub-identity we call ego.

If a few small streams of water remain separate from each other, they don't form a significant body of water. But when these streams began to converge, they form a river, which has a force all its own. Similarly, a few recurrent thoughts and tendencies converge and appear as the sense of individuality we call ego.

The ego is not a separate entity. It is a web of recurrent, closely associated thoughts infused with energy. That web of thoughts and tendencies expresses as our unique personalities.

The ego is neither good nor bad. It is an experience in awareness. Recognizing it is fundamentally no different than recognizing an apple sitting on the kitchen counter. The apparent difference is that the ego feels intensely personal because its story is repeated endlessly over a lifetime.

This sub-identity we call *ego* can go through various stages of development as the body develops through the stages of infant, child, preteen, teenager, young adult, adult, and elder. Whenever the thoughts and tendencies change, we might say, "Joe has changed. He's not who he used to be."

Somewhere along the journey, the series of thoughts we call "Joe" may pause or change, just as new, disruptive thoughts enter: Who am I? What am I? An examination may ensue, wherein a more open, unfettered awareness sees "Joe" as a story within stories.

Who were you before you had a name? What were you before you exhibited likes and dislikes?

The development of the ego is a natural part of human life. It only becomes problematic when development is stunted. If a child doesn't get proper nutrition, the child's bodily development is stunted. Similarly, today's society too often fails to nourish our minds. It serves to build up and concretize stories about who we are and what we need, instead of providing pointers that help us recognize the mechanism that creates the sense of who we are. The result is that the natural unfoldment of the ego is hindered. We are stagnating in a preliminary I-me-mine stage of development. The results are plainly seen in the society around us.

Ironically, the feeling of a separate sub-identity can actually be strengthened when a person starts on what is called a spiritual path. New thoughts are added to the sub-identity, perhaps rejecting one set of behaviors and embracing another set. Yet the key to allowing the ego to loosen, become subtle, and continue along its natural course of unfoldment isn't judging which behaviors are right and which are wrong. Rather, the key to the continued thinning and evolution of the sub-identity is simply seeing its nature. This is neither a uniquely spiritual nor secular practice. It is simply practical.

As we become aware of what we once called the ego, our identity shifts and begins to thin. No further action beyond this awareness is required. In fact, any further action will propagate a new judgement about the ego, adding to its thought pool and creating a new sub-identity.

Identity is a modification of awareness, therefore awareness alone is needed to see through identity.
Most of the problems we see in our society are because of stagnated ego development. When we recognize that the sense of identity is a compelling story, the story automatically becomes less compelling. Creativity oozes out from the previously airtight spaces between thoughts. The personality opens up. Novel solutions are seen. Love, cooperation, and collaboration are valued. Harmony, justice, and opportunity are valued. The sub-identity resumes its practical, functional role as an aspect of a whole community. At the societal level, this would translate into policies and practices that are supportive of the growth of a greater number of people.

Abraham Maslow, in describing the human being's hierarchy of needs, listed "self-actualization" as the pinnacle of life, wherein a person achieves full potential and creativity. This process of actualizing is mirrored by the continued development and thinning of the egoic story, which unfettered awareness sees through ever more clearly.

As an exercise, I invite you to write down a few lines from your core story. Fill in these blanks:

My name is _____

I was born on _____

I love _____

My pet peeve is _____

I wish I could _____

When you've finished filling in these blanks, see if you can describe yourself without referencing any elements of the core story and without emphasizing your physical characteristics. It is not that you are a story, or Joe is a story, but rather that we are much more than the roles we play in our stories. In seeing this, the story itself becomes more enjoyable.

Q&A

1. I always thought the ego was something to get over. I thought I had to control it and tame it.

The idea that we have to control or tame the ego stems from the notion that we are imperfect beings. As individuals, yes, we're imperfect. We're always learning and growing. But our essential nature is perfection itself. As we recognize that underlying nature, the ego is seen within a greater context, within which it has a role that doesn't need to be extinguished.

Seen this way, the ego is neither good nor bad. It's a function of being human. The more we recognize this, the more the idea of wrangling with and controlling the ego begins to fade. Seeing the greater context itself begins to shift the sense of ego.

2. What is it that sees through the ego? Wouldn't that just be another ego? Another identity?

As the mind becomes subtler and subtler, it can recognize the motivation behind its habitual tendencies. It can detect the presence of the ego in the driver's seat, steering our behavior. But even that mind is connected with a subtler sense of ego. Some call this a spiritual ego. It thinks that it has achieved something great in recognizing some of the currents underlying behavior. But this subtle ego too will run up against a wall that it can't see through, can't understand, and can't manage. Perhaps more insight will dawn and the mind might become even subtler. It's like a Russian doll—the mind and ego become subtler and subtler in the process as they approach unfettered consciousness.

Ultimately, the shift to that unfettered consciousness is discontinuous. No amount of steady refinement can bridge the gap between mind and consciousness. This is discussed more in the chapter on enlightenment.

Chapter 4

Where Does Consciousness Go When I Die?

Consciousness is often spoken about as if it's another piece of the puzzle of life, like matter or our thoughts. While it may seem that way, a close analysis reveals that consciousness is of a different order, because everything we know and believe, including perception, science, history, philosophy, and even supernatural phenomena, depends on consciousness being present to begin with. With this in mind, let's address a few questions.

Where does consciousness go when I die?

This question reveals one of the most common misunderstandings about consciousness—that it is fundamentally personal. While consciousness *also* appears as a personal experience (for example, our personal thoughts, emotions, sense of identity), it is also non-personal and non-localized.

A good way to understand this is to look at your last dream. In that dream, you had your own personality, your own brain, and your own body, but the *stuff* those were made of is the same *stuff* that the furniture in the dream was made of, namely your sleeping mind.

Similarly, consciousness appears as the localized personality, but is in no way restricted to a particular type of appearance. All appearances are oscillations or patterns of consciousness.

With this understanding, it is seen that time and space are also appearances of consciousness. So where does consciousness go when I die? It doesn't go anywhere because it hasn't come from anywhere. Every "where" is a location in space and time. What "dies" (or, more precisely, what trans-forms) is a particular pattern of consciousness—what we call "mind," appearing as a body and personality.

Why are we so interested in living longer?

Religion talks about the afterlife. Spirituality talks about immortality. Philosophy talks about the meaning of life. Science investigates how we can extend our lives.

Why the obsession with living longer, living forever, or transcending birth and death altogether? The interest in longer life, heaven, immortality, and supernatural states stems from the deep recognition every human being has that there's more to the picture than the 4-D world. Every human has the capacity for wonder. Regardless of which thought system you subscribe to or don't subscribe to, wonder comes standard. That wonder is an opening to infinity. It hints that beyond that gateway is something beyond imagination, even if we never conceptualize or articulate it as such.

Heaven and immortality are not physical things. They exist in their own way right now, right here, beyond the veil of physicalized perceptions and localized identity. As they are recognized, the interest in them naturally wanes, because they are not somewhere else, some goal to be attained. Paradoxically, the more unreal they seem, the more intriguing they can be, because that means the gap between my perception and reality is great, and so I pant for clarity.

The desire to live longer is an opaque projection of the desire to see this moment fully, clearly.

Does heaven really exist?

Every place that we experience is a mental experience. (This is discussed in greater detail in Part II.) This is very apparent when we analyze all the places we visit in a dream, but it seems to be different now when we're awake. In fact, it is not different. This world we experience is also mental in nature, when viewed from the perspective of consciousness itself, as opposed to the individual mind.

Instead of calling a dream a dream, we can also say it's another dimension of experience. In this waking mental dimension, I am one character, and in other dimension (dream), I might be another character.

If that's true, then a place like heaven (and other places) would also simply be other dimensions. The reason heaven seems magical and perhaps unbelievable is because we are not fully perceiving even this experience of the world we are having now. When we see this world as a bunch of physical things, then the reality of other dimensions of experience that defy what we call physical laws seems unlikely. But if we recognize this world itself as a dimension of experience, then the existence of other dimensions is no longer magical or absurd. It's quite natural.

Is reincarnation real?

Incarnation literally means in-flesh, or in the body. So, an incarnation is when we assume a physical form. Reincarnation would then be leaving one form and taking on another. It would be trans-formation. We already know that energy cannot be created or destroyed. It can only be transferred or changed. But is that true of our bodily and mental forms as well?

This is really a question about memory. Specifically, we're asking: Did I have a form prior to the one I have now?

When you woke up this morning, you didn't feel like you had reincarnated from yesterday because you remembered the form you had yesterday. But what if you didn't remember yourself prior to today? How would you know whether you had reincarnated or simply sustained memory loss? You might believe that reincarnation is absurd, but there would be no way to know without having any memories to draw on.

Generally, a human being's earliest memories are from when we were roughly three to five years old. What happened prior to that is usually unavailable. As a species, we suffer from a massive collective amnesia of our first few years of life, even though events happening during those years shape our experience of life for decades to come. If that's the case, it is equally possible that we are amnestic to events prior to those first few years as well.

Q&A

1. *Are you saying that what we're experiencing right now is just one dimension of the mind?*

Yes. This dimension is the human mind recognizing itself in what we call the "awake" state. The dream state is another dimension of experience. Similarly, there are many dimensions of experience. All of these are aspects of consciousness.

2. *I want to know if reincarnation is real.*

Reincarnation is a way of categorizing experiences of form. We are experiencing form right now—the form of a body. Every night, we drop our association with this form, and every morning, we pick it up again. Reincarnation is another kind of dissociation and association with a body and a particular mind. Because it has to do with changing forms and not that which appears as change (consciousness), reincarnation is not real in the ultimate sense.

Chapter 5

The Three Stages of Meditation

As I was scrolling through my Twitter feed after searching for #meditation, I noticed something. There is a lot of contradictory information out there. One tweet says meditation is about controlling the mind. Another says it's about watching the mind. Yet another says it has nothing to do with the mind. I noticed that when I describe meditation in different contexts, I myself use phrases and descriptions that sound at odds with each other.

Despite all the info I came across, there was one aspect of meditation that nobody was talking about.

First, what is meditation?

Meditation is an introspective technique that increases your awareness of who and what you are, and as a result, of what the world is.

Most people in our society are taught from a young age that they are a body, and perhaps a mind. But we are not taught what the nature of the mind is, what its limits and capabilities are, and how it shapes our identity and experience of the world. We are not taught that the sense of identity we have isn't fixed, even though we all experience the fickleness of identity when we shift into a dream character, or when our identity disappears in deep sleep. All this happens in the dance between mind and the core of our awareness.

Meditation isn't magic. It makes sense: Place more attention on what you are, and you will discover more of what you are. The results are better than any magic trick.

Why is meditation important?

It's important because much of the unhappiness and frustration a person faces is created by a case of mistaken identity. We were told we are so-and-so, and we believed it. But the truth is we are *also* so-and-so, not *only* so-and-so. The rest of our identity is waiting in the background. Recognizing our full identity is like coming home. You know when you're driving home after a really long and exhausting trip, and you're tired, and your back hurts from being in the car so long, and the Cheetos just aren't cutting it, and the song you really want to hear just won't play?

And then... you get home... and flop onto your bed... and just like that... everything shifts. It all seems okay. When you wake up in the morning, everything seems different.

When the case of mistaken identity is seen through, perspective shifts, and things seem okay. Problems don't go away. Instead, they are put in a radically different context.

What are the 3 stages of meditation?

Stage 1: Observing thoughts and feelings

This is often the most difficult stage for someone starting to meditate. Thoughts fly around with dizzying speed. Memories erupt. Frustration abounds...

"Am I doing this right?"

"I'm not doing this right!"

"How the hell do people actually meditate? This is impossible!"

"I will be the only person who never learns to meditate."

"Why did I do this?"

"How am I supposed to control my mind? It controls me!"

If you've had these thoughts, or are having these thoughts, give yourself a pat on the back. These are the symptoms of early success in Stage 1. No, really, I'm not kidding. Everyone has similar thoughts and frustrations.

By taking the time to watch your thoughts and feelings, just as someone might watch a movie, you are making an evolutionary leap. You are starting to learn how the control center works, how your inner GPS navigates.

As Stage 1 progresses, the incessant thoughts and feelings and memories that run together like a thick goo will slowly start to separate. Gaps will appear between them. What do you have to do? Just keep watching the show, nothing else. At some point, you'll notice the gaps as much as you notice the content filling the gaps. That's the beginning of Stage 2.

Stage 2: Observing silence

This stage begins when attention shifts from content (thoughts, feelings, sensations, etc.) to the silent gaps in between the content. You make an intention to ignore the content and instead focus on the silence. You see the canvas instead of the painting. You hear silence instead of music. You attend to the background rather than the foreground.

As Stage 2 progresses, the duration of the gaps will increase. Silence will seem louder than sound. The background will come to the foreground. The busy world of thought content will seem more distant, but still relatable.

A point of clarification. Observing silence doesn't mean you are trying to be silent. You are simply noticing the silence between the episodes of content that play in the mind. Your attention is placed on silence. No effort is needed to increase or manipulate silence, or to change your thoughts.

Sometimes you'll notice silence clearly. Often, you won't. Either one is success, as long as you continue.

This silence is the road home.

Two roads diverged in a wood, and I —
I took the one less traveled by,
And that has made all the difference.
– Robert Frost

Travel the road of silence. It cannot but lead you home.

Stage 3: Losing yourself

This is the stage of meditation that few people talk about. Why not? Because it's not as sexy as the first two stages. You can't force it to happen, and furthermore, you can't *do* anything with it.

Observing thoughts and feelings (Stage 1) can be fun. It can even yield a sense of control.

Observing silence too can be fun (Stage 2). It can give you peace and insight. You may unleash new abilities and talents.

Stage 3 is about one thing: Losing that firm grip on who you knew you were. It's when silence empties itself into the ineffable. There's a shift in the way the individual relates to everything, because the very sense of identity shifts.

This happens when the mind comes home. First, our awareness was on thoughts and emotions. Then, it was on silence. Now, it has passed through silence and rests in itself, by itself. This resting in oneself has a potentiating effect that shifts the sense of identity.

Sometimes, Stage 3 is glossed over by invoking a popular word: enlightenment. Enlightenment is a grand word, but its implications to an individual who wants it may not be so grand.

Think back to the analogy of the weary traveler who finally reaches home and falls into bed. When sleep finally arrives, the traveler loses his/her identity. Another way of saying this is that identity becomes unbounded, instead of remaining bound around the frame of an individual.

What would it be like for the sense of identity to be unbounded even while awake, even while a parcel of infinity continues as a personality in the world? It is unimaginable to the individuated mind, yet every wisdom tradition around the world speaks of it. This is where Stage 3 leads.

Meditation as an activity dissolves itself in Stage 3, because the meditator is seen through in Stage 3.

Where does mindfulness fit into all this?

Some people call Stage 1 mindfulness. Some call Stage 2 mindfulness. It doesn't really matter. As long as the basic progression is understood, you have a good map of meditation. Use the terminology that works for you.

Ultimately, meditation is about you—all of what you are. The technique should be used and understood properly. It is not a cure-all for the personality, though it certainly brings a sense of ease. It is an unveiling of the rest of our identity.

The terrain of consciousness is yours to explore.

Q&A

1. *I try to meditate but I usually fall asleep. What should I do?*

If the mind is not well rested, it will fall asleep during meditation. That's okay. If you can't get to bed earlier, one thing you can do is grab a few minutes of meditation throughout the day. For example, when you get to work, stay in the car for an extra three minutes and dive into yourself. Set the alarm on your phone if you have to. Do the same when you go home. Even a few minutes like this will help recalibrate the mind and help it stay rested. Then you can lengthen the amount of time you meditate without falling asleep.

2. *Meditation is too hard. I can't control my mind.*

Meditation isn't about controlling the mind. The more you struggle with the mind, the more it will struggle back. Recognize that the mind has its ups and downs. It has its periods of activity and periods of rest. That's the nature of the mind. Wanting to change that comes from a sense of self-judgement: *I should be doing better. I can't do this.* In these moments, remind yourself that the point of meditation is not to control the mind. To begin with, let the mind be and simply watch it like an episode of a series. An easy meditation is available at anoopkumar.com/meditate.

Eventually, the mind's ups and downs will naturally even out as it gets the tantrums out of its system. The resulting mind is sometimes referred to as the "controlled" mind, but it is better described as a more restful mind.

3. *I like meditating and find it helpful, but part of me also feels like I'm escaping from the world. There's so much happening in the world. I don't want to retreat from it.*

One way to see meditation is as a process of summoning more of yourself. You are accessing resources that you've always had hidden away in the closet. In the beginning, it can seem like you're running away from the world, but in fact what you're doing is recharging. We all do the same thing when we sleep. We are not running from the world when we sleep. We're merely going to a place that restores us and helps us bring more resources to bear on the next day.

Similarly, meditation helps us bring more resources to the life we live. If we want to apply those resources at work, we can. If we want to apply them at home, we can. It's like acting with more information on hand. In fact, those resources influence the entirety of our life. They can't be restricted to one sphere because they function at a deeper level than that of an individual personality.

As meditation continues, the walls of the mind begin to crumble. The dividing walls between you, me, she, he, and them are seen through. Meditation is then no longer about running away from life because "my life" and what is happening in the world are not different.

4. *I've had many strange experiences in meditation. What do they*

mean? What should I do about them?

Many kinds of experiences can arise in meditation. Some can be pleasant and exhilarating while others can be scary. Often, a person may say, *Okay—that's enough. I'm not going there.*

The mind is unpredictable. Anything that has been stored in the mind in the past may come up in meditation. If you find an experience particularly unsettling, it can be helpful to talk to someone about it rather than trying to deal with it by yourself. If things feel overwhelming, don't push yourself. Take a break. Do something active with your body.

Mystical experiences can also arise. You may develop abilities you didn't have before. You may have flashes of insight. These may happen not only during meditation but even in the course of your day or in dreams.

If such experiences happen, there will be the temptation to interpret their meaning. *What are they trying to tell me?* I would simply say that these are experiences that needed to be released and integrated within you. They're not necessarily saying anything beyond that. At the same time, we don't have to pretend they're not meaningful. They can feel intensely meaningful. Simply recognize that whatever meaning is interpreted is relative to the sense of identity we carry. As the sense of identity becomes subtler, the meanings and even the importance of that meaning will change.

There's nothing in particular one has to do about these experiences. Although they can be unusual compared to the typical experiences we encounter in daily life, they are fundamentally the same: an experience that comes and goes.

5. *I've been meditating for a long time and feel like I'm in a rut. What can I do?*

If you've had a regular meditation practice for a long time, the practice itself can fall into a rut. The mind can become used to swinging in and out of meditation. One way to get out of the rut is to become aware of what your mind is like *before* you start meditating and *after* you finish meditating. In other words, recognize the mind changing from a premeditation state to a meditation state to a post-meditation state. Keep your attention on the shifting states rather than only on the meditation itself. Recognizing this makes the mind broader and subtler. Meditation will no longer be a specific activity to do at a particular time for a particular duration. Rather the mind simply remains meditative—sometimes more active, sometimes less.

Chapter 6

What You Are Is More Than Who You Are

Who am I?

I am <name>.

I am <x> years old.

I am a <profession>.

By continuing to ask, "Who am I?" a person can inquire into the depths of identity. The inquiry is not merely intellectual, although it can be aided by the intellect. The inquiry must be of the very experience or sense of personal identity.

See if you can notice the sense of I-ness now.

Ultimately, this sense of I-ness, or identity, will push up against the boundary that separates me from the world.

This is where it's helpful to ask a subtler question:

What am I?

As long as I am inquiring into *who* I am, there can be a thin psychological film that obscures the view beyond personal identity. To see beyond that film, it can help to look into *what* I am.

What I am no longer has to be about personal identity, because it is not personified. It allows peeks into wherever "I" appears from.

What we are is free, open, gentle, still, aware, boundless, infinite.

At the level of what we are, there is no difference between you, me, and the world. All are apparent outcroppings of infinity.

Chapter 7

Self-Awareness Is Its Own Reward

Is it possible to cure disease by exploring subtler aspects of ourselves? If so, is that the ultimate benefit of self-awareness? Let's explore.

Exploring oneself through some form of introspection increases self-awareness. As self-awareness develops, we become more aware of our triggers and the reasons why we make the choices we make. Often, choosing to remain aware of these triggers also begins the process of defusing them, leading to better choices: better nutrition, movement, and rest—choices that are more in line with our well-being. This is the simplest and most obvious way in which self-awareness can lead to healing.

As self-awareness progresses and the journey into the mind deepens, stress and suppressed emotions start to make their way up and out. These interlopers introduced themselves to us long ago, but perhaps we didn't recognize or want to deal with them at the time. Their cathartic release can ease tension out of the mind and body. Back pain can improve. Headaches can improve. Irritability, anxiety, and depressed moods can improve. More healing occurs. New abilities and old talents may be unearthed.

But self-awareness isn't just about releasing stress. In fact, releasing stress is actually a side effect of self-awareness. As introspection progresses and self-awareness further expands, subtle subjective processes come to light. These subtler aspects of ourselves can unveil new mechanisms of healing.

For the most part, such subtle mechanisms have not been noted by science, primarily because they haven't been objectified enough to be recognized and adequately investigated. The subtler a process is, the more difficult it is to objectively investigate.

Some scientists say there are no such subtle processes—no new self-directed mechanisms of healing waiting to be discovered. If we can't detect something, how could we possibly say it exists? They make a good point. Until enough people recognize such processes and codify them systematically, this will remain a point of contention, with a lot riding on the final answer.

What we do know is the body can heal itself from supposedly incurable conditions, including advanced cancer and heart disease. When this happens, we call it a miracle because we don't know how to initiate the healing process. It seems to just happen (although the evidence for reversing heart disease is strong enough that it is no longer in miracle territory).

Whether such cures are miracles or not, it goes without saying that there is a process by which the body is healing itself. And the very fact that we still have not understood those processes despite the brain power, technology, time, and money we pour into research suggests that those processes may be subtler than we imagine. We may be looking for apples when oranges are the answer. Self-awareness can shed light on this problem.

So far, we've seen that self-awareness can help heal—often in mundane ways, and perhaps in unrecognized ways. Is that all? Is that the Big Deal with self-awareness?

No. Self-awareness is not ultimately about healing a physical or mental process, or about acquiring new abilities, although those may happen. Just as often, they may not. That's why there are many people who may be self-aware, but still have physical and mental afflictions. The one sure healing that self-awareness ultimately brings is that of a sense of completion, of wholeness beyond body and mind, beyond birth and death.

At its core, self-awareness heals a case of mistaken identity. What I thought I once was—a person defined by and confined to a physical body and personality—is no longer a primary identity. The body doesn't go away, the personality doesn't disappear, and wings don't grow on your back, but any sense of incompleteness and lack fades away.

Healing is about being the whole you, not about curing parts of you. That's why self-awareness is its own reward.

Q&A

1. *Can you clarify exactly what you mean by healing?*

The word *heal* is derived from the word *whole*. Therefore, healing is about returning to wholeness, to an ideal. Healing at the level of the body and mind means restoration of function. It occurs as a process in time. Healing at the level of awareness is not a process in time. It's a shift in perspective, or a shift in consciousness. It's not about changing the picture, but rather seeing the very same picture in a new way. Thereafter, the body and mind may or may not change in the way we had once wished, yet they are already seen as whole.

Chapter 8

What Is Enlightenment?

According to the National Institutes of Health, about 20 million adults in the United States alone meditate. Millions more do yoga. Meditation and yoga are now household words. Why have they become so popular?

Meditation and yoga can give us a glimpse of our natural state of awareness. This is different from the state of awareness we have during the course of a typical day. Usually, our awareness takes the form of being an individual, being happy, or being frustrated. Meditation takes us on a journey beyond these states of awareness. Meditation ends in our natural state of being— what is often labeled "enlightenment" or self-realization.

Enlightenment is associated with many misconceptions

1. *Enlightenment means the mind doesn't exist anymore.* False. The mind still functions in enlightenment, but not as something different than consciousness itself. In other words, the apparent duality of mind and consciousness is seen through, just as the apparent duality of matter and mind are seen through. The individual "me" is seen as a superimposition of consciousness on consciousness, rather than as an independently real entity.

2. *Enlightened people never feel angry or sad.* False. Remember that the mind still functions in enlightenment. The mind can feel sad or angry, or any other emotion. However, it doesn't get bogged down in that emotion because the sense of identity has shifted. In fact, later in this chapter, we'll question the very notion of an "enlightened person." The subtler the mind becomes, the

less bogged down it gets. States of mind will come and go, like clouds passing in the sky.

3. *Enlightenment will solve all my problems.* False. What enlightenment does is shift the identity of "me" beyond the sense of individuality. Where does identity go? It doesn't go any particular place, because it wasn't a physical *thing* to begin with. It is merely released from the limitation of individuality. If it goes somewhere or into something, like an expansive, subtle state, recognize that to be a mental state. This shift of identity doesn't mean that the individual's problems disappear, although some problems will no longer be thought of as problems anymore. Rather, they're seen from a much broader perspective which allows new creative solutions.

4. *Enlightenment is a mystical experience.* False. Mystical experiences, intuitions, peak experiences, and states of ecstasy may happen, but these by themselves are not enlightenment. These too are states that come and go.

So then, what will I get out of enlightenment?

What the mind "gets" from enlightenment is the freedom to be itself without judgement. Over the course of our lives, we have modified our behavior innumerable times to fit the shoulds and should-nots of our communities. We have created a dreamlike state (often nightmare-like) to live in. We are told that if we do not behave like others and accept what others accept, then we won't fit in, or we'll act irresponsibly. When the walls of individuality fall off the mind, such controlling ideas and self-judgements fall away. i makes way for I. Notice the mind isn't really getting anything in this process. It's merely losing its misconceptions and self-imposed limitations.

Who gets enlightened?

There are three answers to this question.

1. Whoever honestly and diligently investigates their own identity through any form of introspection is on the path of enlightenment. Honesty means you are true to your own quest. You cannot fully accept (or reject) somebody else's words, no matter who they are, until they are true (or false) for you. This means you must be able to investigate any hypothesis you encounter, no matter how outlandish it may seem, using your own experience as data. Diligence means you continue with your investigation until all questions either disappear or become irrelevant, and freedom becomes your nature. Honesty and diligence are indispensable.

The investigation of identity does not have to be highly philosophical. You don't have to inquire, "Who am I?" over and over again. You may begin with the insight, "This world is like a movie!" or "What a crazy world!" When you dive (introspect) into that subjective experience, you are in fact investigating your identity, your *i*. Your investigation may or may not feel intellectual. The biggest questions in life, such as, "Who am I? What is the nature of this world? What happens at birth and death?" are not to be answered by books or concepts, although these can help point the way. Such questions are internal, experiential investigations.

2. It is also true that some people appear to spontaneously realize their true nature, without much investigation. This is like saying the first snowfall of the winter is a spontaneous occurrence. It is true that at one moment there is no snow, and in the next moment there is snow falling. But it is also true that the entire range of seasons from spring to summer to fall to winter was necessary to create the first snowflake. When we look at enlightenment as an event, it can appear spontaneous. But the subjective unfolding of the mind had been in process long before, unrecognized. Even after such an apparently spontaneous

experience, there is a period of settling and integrating that occurs.

3. Many people today say that enlightenment is when consciousness wakes up to itself. However, consciousness itself, being infinite, seamless, and dimensionless, has no need to wake up. (I'm using the word consciousness here synonymously with awareness and being.) In fact, we can even say it *cannot* wake up because it is already awake-ness, so to speak. A flower in full bloom cannot bloom. A person with open eyes cannot open their eyes. Similarly, consciousness can't become more conscious, or enlightened.

What gets enlightened is the mind. The reason there is so much confusion about this is because when the mind gets enlightened, the first-person sense of individuality in the mind loosens. Therefore, we generally don't see enlightened people saying, "I am enlightened," since the sense of "I" is no longer restricted to the individual mind. The mind is enlightened, yes, but "I," as consciousness, is not. This is the essence of self-realization.

Consciousness is not enlightened; it is ever awake. Individual identity is not enlightened; it loosens. The mind is enlightened, or more precisely, is always enlighten-ing, characterized by the shift from a personal mind to a trans-personal mind as the individual sense of identity is seen through. Therefore, the journey of the mind as a subtle, ever-refining, trans-personal experience continues with enlightenment, and consciousness remains as it ever was, beyond time and beyond change. Seen in this way, enlightenment is not a particular event, nor the achievement of any individual.

What is the "light" of enlightenment?

The light of enlightenment is two-fold.

1. The light is metaphorical: a lightness of being. Imagine walking around for a year carrying a hundred-pound weight

around your shoulders. Your back hurts. Your shoulders hurt. You're sore. You're cranky. Worst of all, this seems to be a normal part of life, because everyone else is also carrying a hundred-pound weight. Further imagine that you don't recognize where this tremendous burden you feel is coming from. You think it's just a part of you.

One day, in the midst of your misery, the weight falls off your shoulders. The entire load falls to the ground with a resounding thud. You look down, see the massive iron weight, and in a flash you recognize the truth behind all that suffering, accompanied by an indescribable relief and joy.

That amazing, indescribable lightness you feel is akin to the lightness of enlightenment. In enlightenment, the weights that are dropped are the accrued self-judgements and misconceptions of the mind. As with any amazing experience, the thrill of the event wanes as the mind adjusts to a new way of experiencing the world. The contrast of heaviness and lightness fades. The lightness of being simply becomes being.

2. The light is literal. There are two kinds of light in the literal sense: light that is seen (known to science as particle and wave) and light that sees, or is self-effulgent (unknown to science). Consciousness is self-effulgent. It requires nothing else to be conscious. That self-effulgence is what expresses as the mind and world. All our perceptions, indeed everything we know, is known in and as the light of self-effulgent consciousness, even when the mind doesn't recognize it.

When first-person individuality loosens, identity reverts back to the natural being of consciousness. With this shift, our natural self-effulgence is once more recognized. Self-effulgence then shines as the world of subjective and objective experiences — mind, body, and world.

When is enlightenment complete?
Consciousness itself never changes. Mind, on the other hand,

always changes. Therefore, enlightenment cannot have a point of completion relative to form because form (the mind) is always refining itself. Completion can only be described as non-dual consciousness—the I beyond *i*—in which there is no second, no first, no other.

In this context, one has to question what in fact an "enlightened person" is. We see another person's body and mind and tend to project our own sense of identity onto that person and say she or he is enlightened or not, whereas enlightenment challenges the very notion of a separate she or he.

Q&A

1. *I thought enlightenment was about getting supernatural abilities.*

As the mind becomes subtler, the veil that separates consciousness itself from our sense of individuality and the sense of an external world dissipates. This allows the personality to open up and access more of the creativity that has remained latent for so long, which sometimes expresses as new talents and abilities. Any such ability is itself an expression of the mind, and growing attached to that ability will ultimately stunt the progression of the mind. The key is to use what abilities are available while recognizing them as tools rather than goals.

2. *Why do you say the mind continues in enlightenment? I've heard spiritual teachers say that enlightenment is about transcending the mind.*

"Transcending the mind" needs to be understood in the right context. Transcending, in this case, refers to seeing beyond the mind. What is it that would see beyond the mind? Ultimately, not the mind itself. The phrase "transcending the mind" refers to self-awareness or consciousness beyond the mind. It does not mean the mind ceases to function. Consciousness has no quarrel with any particular experience. It is not contradicted by any experience, including the very denial of consciousness, which would be a thought within consciousness itself.

3. *Why do you say there are no enlightened people? What about Jesus, Buddha, and Krishna?*

What I'm suggesting is the very notion of an enlightened person appears real only if we project our own sense of individuality on someone else. Another way to say this is to consider that no *individual* is enlightened. The mind simply grows subtler, loses its walls, and increasingly reflects the light of consciousness. That mind is no longer bound to an individual identity.

When we refer to Jesus, Buddha, Krishna, and others, including many today who are living inconspicuous lives, we refer to them as individual people because that's how we see ourselves. That individuality is something we lend to them just as we lend it to ourselves. When we recognize that our own individuality is something we have borrowed that is not representative of most of what we are, then that same recognition is immediately seen in all "others" as well. At that point, the usefulness of the notion of enlightenment wanes. Instead of saying so-and-so is enlightened and so-and-so is not enlightened, we might simply say *consciousness is*.

Chapter 9

Our Nature Is Simplicity Itself

If we went beyond thinking, feeling, and sensing right now, what would remain?

I invite you to try this exercise for a moment. Close the eyes, relax, and see if you notice the still, silent center within you.

Notice the balance and equipoise.

Notice the stillness.

Activities may still be surging around you. Your mind may indeed be thinking and feeling. That's not a problem.

Notice that the stillness always remains, even as activity continues. Sometimes it's in the foreground. Sometimes it's forgotten in the background.

Now let yourself go into that stillness. Fall into it, gently, without an agenda.

It deepens. It permeates the mind. Boundaries melt.

You are falling unto your self.

This stillness is the gateway to a part of ourselves that our minds obscure. The gate is plain. There are no fancy markings. It is so simple that it is often missed.

As one approaches the gate and glides in, a band might play. Fireworks may go off. Movies might run. All of these may come, and therefore all of them will go.

Your true nature is profoundly simple and simply profound. It is not found in the complexity of philosophy, the rigor of strenuous practice, or the measurements of science, though the mind may enjoy chomping on these.

It is found by falling in love with the simplicity we all share.

Chapter 10

Waking, Dreaming, and Sleeping Happen in You

Many years ago, *Science* magazine declared that one of the most important and unanswered questions in science is: *What is the universe made of?* Today, we still don't know the answer. Part of the problem is that we, as human beings, are part of the very universe we are trying to understand. Therefore, it goes without saying that if we don't understand our own nature, we are likely to misunderstand the nature of the universe.

To fully understand ourselves, we must look at the entire breadth of our life experiences. Usually, this doesn't happen. Most of our analysis happens from one state of mind—the waking state, which we are in right now. All that we know about perception and reasoning, we know based on our waking experience. Since we don't conduct scientific experiments in our sleep or in our dreams, those two crucial states of human experience don't contribute much to our understanding of the universe.

The dream and deep sleep states have something important to teach us. If we want to know the nature of the universe and our own nature, we have to consider *all* the data we have access to, not just the data we accrue while having a waking experience.

The Dream State

Within a dream, we assume an identity, operate in an environment, and are subject to apparent cause and effect. The content of the dream appears to be made of matter. You and I, as characters in that dream, cycle through successes and failures, ups and downs. What is the nature of that dream world and what can it tell us about the universe?

A close analysis of the dream state tells us that what we consider to be matter within a dream is nothing but mind on waking up from the dream. What we consider to be an enemy in our dream is nothing but our own nature as the mind. You, as the mind, become both the hero and the villain in the dream, not to mention the battlefield itself. Within the dream, such insights are not revealed. One has to become wise to the dream's nature to see them. The implications of this on our current experience in the waking state can be startling.

But even an analysis of the dream state is not enough. What about that great mystery we call the deep sleep state? The mystery that both scientists and sages wonder about? What secrets might it whisper about the nature of the universe and ourselves?

The Mystery of Deep Sleep

Deep sleep is a unique state of experience. It is the experience of *no-thing*. In deep sleep, the individual mind withdraws all its activities and returns to its dormant form, just as a turtle withdraws from activity by pulling its limbs into its shell. In its dormant form, the mind no longer projects any experience. It rests in undifferentiated potentiality, replenishing itself for the next outing, whether that be as an episode of the dream state or an episode of the waking state. When the mind wakes up, it recognizes it is replenished and is able to say, "I slept well."

When I sleep, the world disappears to me, but is still present to you. My mind does not project since it is dormant, while yours still projects. On the other hand, when you sleep, your mind stops projecting its interpretation of the world, while my mind continues interpreting a world.

As long as we are in deep sleep, we are in a state of indeterminate identity. I can't say I am Anoop while I'm asleep. Anoop is a costume I don only upon waking up. In fact, the very notion of a particular, localized, personal "I" is lost in deep sleep. The reason identity is indeterminate in deep sleep is because not only does the mind not project the personal identity "Anoop," its dormant state also veils the underlying consciousness that is present. It is this underlying consciousness that replenishes the mind when it sleeps.

This is key to recognize: The mind sleeps. The mind dreams. The mind wakes up in the morning. You are the underlying consciousness that illumines these states. In the previous sentence, "You" does not refer to a personal you. It is not the individual you, nor the individual me. It is the non-dual itself, beyond individual, world, and mind. That non-dual "You" assumes the identity of an individual in the waking and dream states. And it un-assumes it in deep sleep.

When you sleep and I sleep, we go to the exact same "place." It's not a physical location of course. You may go to sleep in France and I may go to sleep in the United States, but when we sleep, we leave the mental projection of a physical world and go to exactly the same "place"—the non-projected domain of non-dual consciousness. It's just that we typically don't know it because the dormant mind's *habit* of projection veils the underlying consciousness even though it is not actively projecting when we sleep.

When the habit of mental projection is recognized by the even subtler mind, the tendency to get lost in the projection diminishes. As this happens, the veil of the mind thins, and it no longer hides the underlying consciousness that is ever-present in waking, dreaming, and sleeping. When the veil reaches a threshold of becoming sufficiently thin, what was previously known as deep sleep simply turns into deep rest.

Thereafter, there is only projection and non-projection. Projection includes the waking and dreaming (and daydreaming) states happening during deep rest, whereas non-projection is deep rest without projection. Sleep as it was once known is converted into timeless rest, beyond states of mind. In other words, sleep is only sleep so long as the dormant mind veils consciousness. When it no longer veils consciousness, sleep becomes timeless deep rest.

All three of these states—waking, dream, and deep sleep—must be understood to know the nature of reality, the nature of the universe, and the nature of ourselves, because each has its own unique vantage point on the sense of identity and the experience of what the world is.

How Do We Get There?

Sink into the silence of meditation. (If you're not sure how to start, visit anoopkumar.com/meditate.) Release any judgement from the mind. Allow it to exhaust itself. As you sink deeper, know that the silence that becomes you is connected to the silence that swallows the mind in deep sleep. This may not be apparent at first, but with practice, the mind will let go of its misconceptions.

There is no new knowledge to gain. There are only misconceptions to release.

Ultimately, there is no fundamental difference between waking, dreaming, and deep sleep. All three involve the appearance and disappearance of experiences, like waves in an ocean. Knowing this is possible when one recognizes oneself as the ocean instead of a particular wave. The ocean represents reality, the nature of the universe, and our own essential nature. They are one and the same.

We are consciousness itself, which appears in part as waking, dream, and deep sleep states. The universe too is no-thing other than this consciousness—our very own nature—appearing as mind and matter.

Q&A

1. *Are you saying that we are currently in a dream?*

What we are experiencing now in this waking state is *like* a dream in that it is made of the same substance a dream is made of—consciousness. In a dream, consciousness fluxes as the mind, and that mind is interpreted by the characters in the dream as a physical world. The same is true in this waking state.

2. *Can you comment on what's happening when I daydream?*

A daydream is a good experience to analyze. You exist simultaneously as two characters—the daydreamer and the character in the dream. It's as if there are two "you's," and in fact there are. You exist at two different levels of identity simultaneously. But if you're totally engrossed in the daydream, you will forget your daydreamer identity. And once you're completely identified as the daydreamer, the daydream itself will stop. The experience of a daydream requires both identities to exist simultaneously. Similarly, the experience you are having now requires multiple levels of identity to exist. It's just that we tend to forget all but the outermost layers of identity due to habit.

3. *Is it possible to be awake while asleep?*

At face value, being awake while asleep is a contradiction, but let's examine this more closely. Sleep is for the mind. When the mind sleeps, it no longer projects. As long as we define being awake as experiencing projection (meaning experiencing a world of separate things, people, etc.) being awake and being asleep are at odds. Therefore, an individual, which itself is a projection, cannot be awake while asleep. But if awakeness is consciousness itself beyond the local, individual mind, then awakeness and sleeping are not at odds. The individual sleeps and wakes up, but consciousness ever is, neither waking nor sleeping.

Chapter 11

How Do I Experience Oneness with Consciousness?

The key to experiencing oneness with consciousness is allowing the mind to settle and become subtler, which can be facilitated to some degree through practice. We'll explore how to do that at the end of this chapter, but first, let's learn more about what happens in the process.

When the mind is subtle, it is able to recognize the apparent difference between itself and consciousness. Until then, the two are often confused and a case of mistaken identity happens.

The apparent difference between mind and consciousness has to be not just an intellectual understanding, but a direct perception. For that perception to be clear, reflection, meditation, and other practices are helpful. Each person will be unique in their practice. It's popular now to suggest that no practice or preparation is needed to know oneself, and that may seem true in some cases. It is possible to glimpse reality without practice, but who wants only glimpses? Without the mind being subtle, it is easy to misunderstand new experiences, get sidetracked, or stagnate.

As the mind becomes subtler, it progresses through stages of understanding. The following can be used as points for reflection and contemplation.

1. *What we call the body is actually an aspect of our personal mind.*

What we call "me" and "you" are personal, individual minds. The outer layer of the personal mind is what we call the body. The inner layer includes more subtle aspects, such as thoughts, feelings, desires, and the sense of localized identity. Therefore, what we call the body is itself an aspect of the personal mind. It is a representation of the personal mind. This stage of understanding is important to get beyond the first veil of dualism, which is the false idea that the physical body is somehow separate and different from mind.

2. *What we call my mind and your mind (which includes our bodies) are parts of the one total mind that contains all experiences of all sentient beings.*

I don't have access to all your experiences, just as you don't have access to all my experiences. Similarly, we don't have access to the experiences of a grasshopper or an elephant. This means that there is some sort of boundary around our personal minds that keeps them separate.

My sense of identity is localized to my thoughts, my feelings, and my body. But remember that the sense of identity is fickle. In a dream, my identity shifts from this mind to the dream mind. When I sleep, identity disappears altogether. So even the sense of my-ness in the form of my mind and my experiences is itself an aspect of the mind. The boundary that separates me, you, the elephant, and the sofa in the living room is mental in nature. It is an appearance like everything else.

This stage of understanding is important to get beyond the second veil of dualism, which is the false idea that my mind is somehow fundamentally different from your mind, other minds, and the apparent things in those minds. Beyond the sense of personal identity, we are one organism, one mind filtering through individual lenses, just as the dream-mind appears as different characters, objects, and scenes.

3. *The one total mind that contains all possible experiences is an appearance of consciousness.*

Think of a movie. When a movie is projected, all the characters and drama of the movie are nothing but light arranged in different forms. There is no reality to the movie, indeed there is no movie at all, other than the light. If light is removed, the movie, the characters, the drama—all of it is literally nonexistent. Along the same lines, what is the light that refracts as all mental experiences of the one mind—personal and impersonal, human and not human, including the subset of "physical" experiences? That light is the self-effulgent light of consciousness.

Consciousness is infinitely more than what it appears as, just as the light of the projector is not depleted in any way by the movie that it appears as. The light remains untouched by the happenings in the movie, yet from a limited perspective it seems to take on limitation as characters, scenes, drama.

Even if there were no movie playing (if there were no mental film), the light would still be as it is. The light is utterly independent of the film and the movie, yet the movie is entirely dependent on the light. Similarly, consciousness is entirely independent of any and all minds, such as mine and yours and the one total mind, yet all minds are entirely dependent upon consciousness.

So how do I experience this?
1. Begin with a practice of meditation. If you are not sure of how to begin meditating, there is a simple, mind-clearing meditation available at anoopkumar.com/meditate.

2. Reflect on the three points above. Think about them and churn your ideas, then write your thoughts down in a journal. The thoughts don't have to be "good" or pretty. They don't have to be consistent. They can be full of doubt. Putting them down on paper helps to crystallize the doubt so that it can be easily shattered.

3. Try to reconcile what you've understood with your living experience, not just in meditation, but also in daily life.

4. Repeat steps 1 through 3.

As the mind becomes subtler, it will bring confusion and repressed experiences to the surface, just as when we knead dough, the individual lumps are more distinctly felt. How each "lump" is engaged is up to each person. Sometimes, talking to a friend can help. Sometimes, it may be physical exercise or a change in the food we eat. Other times, it may be spending time in nature, or simply taking a few easy, full breaths.

These are the personalized aspects of the journey. Old beliefs will dissipate, stagnant emotions will bubble up, and everything we've wanted to avoid will eventually meet us face to face. It's important to be clear about this and not imagine that we can leapfrog these experiences in the hope of some otherworldly revelation. Revelations will happen, but they won't substitute for the benefits of clarifying the mind.

Begin with Step 1.

Q&A

1. *Do I really have to think about all this stuff to experience oneness?*

Oneness is not about thinking or intellectual understanding. However, for a person who wants to understand the nature of this world and how it relates to the experience of an individual identity, the points in this chapter can be helpful. It can help wean a mind that is enmeshed in an incomplete understanding of the world. That weaning helps the mind to rest, become subtler, and have a clearer view of what's happening.

2. *Is oneness the same as consciousness?*

Oneness refers to the experience of non-difference or unity while also recognizing multiplicity. Consciousness is therefore sometimes referred to as a state of oneness. But if we are to be more precise, consciousness is not exactly oneness, but rather non-duality. This is elaborated upon in Part III.

Part II

The World Isn't What You Think It Is

Chapter 12

A Closer Look at Perception

What's happening right now seems pretty straightforward. You're looking at the shapes on this page that we call words, and your brain is then interpreting those shapes to give them meaning.

Let's take a closer look at this process.

This page is shaped as a rectangle. How is that you see this rectangle?

- The first step in visual perception is that the ambient light around you reflects off this rectangular page and enters your eye.
- The second step is that the reflected light is absorbed by your retina, which then generates an electrical signal that it sends to your brain.
- The third step is that the brain interprets that electrical signal into an image in the visual field.

Only after this electrical signal is interpreted into an image in the visual field do you "see" this rectangular page out in front of you. So, this page that you see as well as these words are interpretations of the brain that are cast into the visual field. We don't see the world as it is, we see the human nervous system's interpretation of the world—a virtual reality, a kind of waking dream. In fact, the eye processes only a narrow range of wavelengths of light, from about 400 to 700 nanometers. This means that most of the visual data that is available is not collected by our eyes. Furthermore, even the data that is collected is not directly seen or recognized, but rather interpreted.

Now we come to a fundamental question: What does the world look like prior to interpretation? What is *actually* here, appearing as this page to your human nervous system? We said in Step 1 that light was reflecting from this page to your eyes. But actually, that's not true. The "page" that we are referring to is post-interpretation and not yet available in Step 1. So, what is actually here?

And how about the room around you? How about all the objects around you? How about the bodies of the people around you? How about your own body? These too must be interpretations of what is here, and subsets of what is here, but not nearly what is objectively here, nor all of what is here. How might a bat, which has a different nervous system and uses echolocation to perceive the world, interpret this very page?

The basic mechanism of human perception is essentially the same for the eye, ear, nose, tongue, and skin. The first step differs depending on the organ, but the second and third steps will be similar. For example, the eardrum receives vibrations in the air, then the cochlea of the inner ear converts those vibrations into an electrical signal which it sends to the brain. The tongue contacts particles of food, then the taste buds send an electrical signal to the brain.

We are perceiving an interpreted world. This applies to not only this page you are seeing, but everything you perceive.

So, what is this world prior to interpretation? Who or what are you, prior to interpretation?

Q&A

1. *Are you saying that the eyes don't see, but rather the brain sees?*

The eyes are like cameras that focus outward. We see through our eyes, but it is the brain that interprets. That interpretation is what we subjectively experience as an apparently objective world. The experience is mental.

It's not that the brain sees, but rather that the brain itself is a sight that is seen. More on this in the next chapter.

Chapter 13

A Tale of Two Minds

In the last chapter, we saw that this world is an interpretation of a particular nervous system—your human nervous system. If that's true, then even what we call the brain is an interpreted perception. The soft, fleshy, grey, cauliflower-like brain we know and love is a composite of perceptions.

This leaves us with a major problem. If all that I perceive is an interpretation, including my brain, then what does the word *physical* mean? The page you see in front of you is not supposed to be an interpretation. We were told in school that it exists objectively in front of you and independent of you. This is a position consistent with the philosophy of materialism. But on close analysis, we see that the interpretation of an independent physical world is exactly that—an interpretation. This brings us to two different perspectives on what the mind is.

The materialist mind recognizes a world that is independent of the interpreting nervous system. In other words, to such a mind, this page would exist as it appears now regardless of whether it is being interpreted. It's important to recognize that there are degrees of materialism, as there are with any perspective. For example, I may recognize a physical world that is independent of interpretation, but I may also appreciate that the same world probably looks different to another species. The apparent inconsistency in that perspective would then be pushed beyond the veil of perception by suggesting that there is still some underlying physical world that is absolutely independent of perception which is being interpreted differently by different species.

Since the world is physical to the materialist mind, then the mind is everything else that is left over, namely, our thoughts and feelings. The materialist mind is the personal, separate mind. It is each individual's personal thoughts and feelings.

The idealist mind recognizes that the world we perceive is an interpretation that is dependent on the interpreter. There is no independent world out there, but rather only one that depends on the mechanism of interpretation. Therefore, the idealist mind recognizes all perceptions, including our bodies, as the mind.

Note that the full perspective of idealism assimilates the perspective of materialism. The world can be mental, but that doesn't mean you and I can't have apparently separate thoughts and feelings. There can be different levels of mind.

One fact holds true regardless of whether we are seeing the world through the materialist mind or through the idealist mind. Either way, we are recognizing an interpretation. One interpretation is broader and includes the other, but both are still interpretations. If we are to see the world through the idealist mind, we would still be left with the question: What is it that is appearing as this mind?

Q&A

1. *What do you mean when you use the word "mind"?*

By *mind*, I mean any experience that changes, which is pretty much every experience. I am using the word *mind* to indicate that the world we perceive is a world primarily of experiences, not of independent things. Because we inter-subjectively agree on those experiences, we have also agreed to consider them as independent *objects*, like a brain or a tree. However, on close analysis, we can recognize that the existence of an object without an interpreting instrument is merely conceptual.

2. *Doesn't the success of science prove that materialism is correct? If the world were mental, how would science be so successful?*

This question is answered in more detail in a subsequent chapter. For now, note that the world being mental doesn't have to mean it is in my mind or your mind. Our individual minds are subsets of a greater, total mind. The discoveries of science are consistent with this.

3. *If the brain is a composite of perceptions, then what is perceiving the brain?*

The mind perceives itself in the form of a brain. We have been educated to believe that the mind is dependent on the brain, but in fact it's the other way around. Mind can exist independent of the brain, but not so the other way around.

4. *Isn't the brain needed for an organism to survive?*

The mind is needed for an organism to survive. That mind sometimes appears as a brain as well, but sometimes doesn't. A bacterium, for example, does not have a brain. Viruses also don't have a brain. Yet, bacteria and viruses are among the best on the planet at reproducing and ensuring their survival. On a larger scale, jellyfish also don't have brains. Yet they swim, find food and assimilate it, and, as we well know, sting when threatened.

Chapter 14

Where Is This Experience Happening?

In November 2017, I had the opportunity to have a conversation with Dr. Deepak Chopra on the topics of healing, consciousness, and the nature of reality.

One of the questions he asked was: *Where is this experience we are having now happening?*

At first, the answer seems like an easy one. The experience we were having—two people conversing in front of an audience—was happening in a room near Broadway in Manhattan. I could've easily answered, "New York City."

Similarly, the experience you are having reading these words is also happening in a physical location. Easy answer, right?

Maybe not.

Let me add a little context. Prior to this question, Deepak and I had already discussed that all physical locations, such as New York City, are structured in space. So, the question Deepak was really asking was, *Where is space located?*

This is a decidedly tougher question, and there is no answer that everyone will agree on. A physicist might answer that space formed with the Big Bang 13.7 billion years ago, but that still doesn't tell us what the preconditions of space were. A mathematician might suggest that the space we know can be traced to an abstract vector space known as Hilbert space. But then where is Hilbert space?

The reason science doesn't have an answer to this question is because it is trying to define space independent of mind. The simple answer to the question of where Hilbert space is located is that it is in the mind. Yet this answer seems insufficient. Why?

We are used to thinking that the mind is exclusively related to the brain, and therefore that the mind is located in the head.

Hilbert space couldn't possibly be located in the head of just one person, right?

It's a reasonable question, but its premise is wrong. The mind is not located in the head, and is not exclusively related to the brain. This is a common misconception that is taught from grade school through medical school. If you observe the behavior of cells distributed throughout the body, you will see mind-like behavior that includes communication with other cells, eating, drinking, and going through an entire life cycle. These mind-like cells constitute the human body, yet they don't have a brain per se.

The mind is not localized in the brain. Rather, the brain is a partial representation of the mind.

This means that what we call the body is the physicalized aspect of the mind, which is not restricted to either a brain or a body, an observation that is consistent with the philosophies of idealism and non-duality.

If we observe the Earth as a whole, we will also see mind-like behavior. The sun rises and sets, the seasons come and go, and civilizations develop and perish. Similar processes can be seen at the cosmic scale with the birth and death of stars. What if all these processes were the activity of mind—not my mind or your mind per se, but the greater mind, of which yours and mine are individuated aspects?

If we can agree that this is possible, as more scientists are doing, then we can make a daring hypothesis: *What we call space and time are aspects of the mind.* Anything we can see, smell, hear, taste, touch, and conceive of is the mind. In its most simple form, the mind is what we conceive of as space and time, which self-modifies as physicalized objects. Take a look around you now, including at the objects in the room and your body. All this is the mind, of which your personal mind of thoughts and feelings is a subset.

The mind begins when foci develop in consciousness, which

is otherwise without boundaries and therefore infinite. When the condition of individuality sets in, multiple foci develop: me/you (localized identity), here/there (space), now/then (time). These foci are the grid on which we interpret the world.

And now we can answer the question: *Where is this experience we are having now happening?*

1. Physical experiences are in space and time.
2. Space and time are in the mind, which appears as physicalized forms and experiences (like the one you're having now).
3. The mind is in consciousness.

Q&A

1. *If physical experiences are in space, space is in the mind, and the mind is in consciousness, then is there any real difference among all these?*

Fundamentally, there is no difference. In fact, this is exactly what the philosophy of non-duality suggests. All appearances are at the surface level when our awareness has identified itself with a particular body. Even the ever-changing mind is recognized only at the level of the mind. At the same time, we can still use concepts like physical, mental, space, and time to navigate our daily experience. We need them to communicate.

2. *You mentioned that cells are mind-like in their behavior. Are you saying that cells are examples of the mind in action?*

Yes, cells are activities of the mind. I don't mean that they are parts of your or my personal mind. They are a mind unto themselves, part of a hierarchical mental structure. All human cell-minds are part of the human organism-mind, which is part of the greater mind.

Chapter 15

Misunderstandings About Consciousness

Misunderstanding #1: The scientific evidence supports the idea that the brain creates consciousness, and therefore that consciousness is not primary.

In a recent conversation, a neuroscientist made the following argument to me: Since evidence shows we can create changes in mental experience by activating or deactivating areas of the brain, it means the brain is causing changes in consciousness. Therefore, the brain (matter) is primary and consciousness is secondary.

At first glance, this may seem like a compelling argument. But on closer inspection, we see that the cited evidence is also entirely consistent with the view that consciousness is primary. If consciousness is primary, then what we call the brain is also a mental experience, a partial representation of local mental processes (such as personality and body). From this perspective, changing the brain simply means changing aspects of the mind. We would definitely expect changes in one aspect of the mind (brain) to reflect in another aspect of the mind (subjective experience), because they are not fundamentally different to begin with.

So why is this misunderstanding believed so strongly? One reason is that many who conduct these experiments implicitly believe in dualism — namely, that there is a physical world and a separate mental world, based on their experience of the world through a mind that is strongly identified with the body. Investigating that belief and seeing how evidence might truly influence it is as much a matter of philosophy (ontology) and self-reflection as it is of science, yet our schools generally don't teach such a balanced approach. Hence, we see many well-known public figures, including scientists and professors, who present this unexamined belief as fact, with a legion of unsuspecting students following suit.

The cited evidence is consistent with both consciousness being primary and matter being primary.

Misunderstanding #2: If you say consciousness is primary, then you are suggesting that this whole world is happening in my head.

This is the allegation of solipsism. The misunderstanding again first presumes a fundamental difference between brain and mind, and then deduces that since the brain is in the head, the entire world of mental experience is also in the head. What I'm saying is that consciousness is fundamental and that the brain (a local reflection of a local personality in consciousness) is an experience in consciousness.

Consciousness is not mine or yours; it is the nature of reality, just as consciousness is the nature of dream, in which individual characters with brains can appear. Therefore, the brain is not needed for consciousness in general, although it certainly appears in strong association with a local identity (mind) like you and me. The world is mental, even if my brain isn't perceiving it.

Another way of seeing this is to recognize that the mind is the primary organ of experience, not the brain. However, that mind wouldn't be my mind or your mind, but rather the universe (or all universes) as mind, of which my mind and your mind are localized processes.

Misunderstanding #3: If this is all a dream, why should we bother?

I'm not saying this waking experience is a dream. I'm saying that whatever this universe of stuff is made of, it's the same stuff that a dream is made of, namely consciousness. As such, it appears as a dream appears, but it is not a dream.

There is a continuity to this waking experience that is generally not present to the same extent in episodic dreams. We still have responsibilities. We still have the ability to improve the quality of our lives and the lives of others. And an important aspect of that is recognizing what we are and what this world is more clearly.

Misunderstanding #4: Matter can't be made of consciousness because we already know it's made of particles.

If I research what my hand is made of, I would find that it's made of muscles, bones, and tendons. A chemist might answer differently and say that it's actually made of carbon, hydrogen, and nitrogen. A physicist might disagree with both and say that the hand is made of elementary particles. Of course, all three would be right, depending on the scale we are looking at.

A closer look reveals that none of these answers tells us what the hand fundamentally is; they only describe what the hand looks like at smaller scales. In other words, the hand is a thing, and so are muscles, carbon atoms, and elementary particles. But what is a thing, fundamentally? This is where consciousness fills out the picture.

In a dream, a dream-scientist could study a dream-hand and still find dream-muscles, dream-atoms, and dream-elementary particles, yet it's obvious that all those levels of structure are still nothing but consciousness appearing as forms at different scales. Importantly, the scientist that is studying the structures is also made of the same stuff. As a hypothesis, consider that the same might be happening right now.

All things are objects of our perception. Even our own bodies and minds are objects of our perception. Consciousness is that which modifies itself as both the observing scientist and the hand that is observed. It modifies itself as the individual you and these words you are reading. Take this as a hypothesis and your own mind as the laboratory.

Misunderstanding #5: Even if consciousness is primary, it doesn't matter. It doesn't change anything.

The more we recognize ourselves as a dance of consciousness, or consciousness reflected upon itself, the more we move toward self-love, peace, and joy. I'm not saying it's impossible to experience these without realizing the primacy of consciousness, but I am saying that there is a limit to how deeply these experiences can unfold as long as our psyche is split into two parts—mental and "physical."

This unnatural mental schism engenders an underlying anxiety and fear that perpetually runs in the background of the mind. At the deepest level, we know something is missing, that something doesn't fit. Recognizing the radical incompleteness of the stories we've been told is the beginning of healing that schism and unleashing the full scope of the mind.

There are many more reasons to consider the primacy of consciousness, including

- It's simultaneously the simplest and most comprehensive theory of the nature of reality.
- It will lead to new scientific discoveries. (The primacy of consciousness is pro-science, which is too often lost on those defending the matter-first perspective.)
- It will lead to the development of more powerful technologies. (It can be argued that perhaps it is good we don't have a deeper understanding of the nature of reality given that the knowledge can easily be misused.)

Misunderstanding #6: This is too complex and convoluted.

The radically incomplete stories we've been told are much more convoluted than the idea that consciousness is primary, which is the simplest and most comprehensive theory of the nature of reality. The primacy of consciousness is recognizable in the early stages of a lifetime, before we even learn to assign it a label. It's only later that we reify the stories we are told into concepts of reality. Take the primacy of consciousness as a hypothesis and begin experimenting.

Chapter 16

Scientists Are Metaphysicians

Merriam-Webster defines metaphysics as "a division of philosophy that is concerned with the fundamental nature of reality and being and that includes ontology, cosmology, and often epistemology." In other words, metaphysics studies questions such as

- What is nature of this universe?
- What am I?
- How do we know what we know?

At first glance these questions may seem hopelessly abstract. But in fact, such questions are not born in our intellects; they're merely intellectual formulations of a deeper intuition that there is much more to know. Children have the same intuition, but because it hasn't been formalized, they may express it through art, emotion, stories, silence, or in different words. Therefore, it often goes unrecognized. That same intuition is what drives the activity of science, which also seeks to know the nature and behavior of the world around us.

Metaphysics as a whole doesn't assume that this world of perceptions you and I are experiencing right now (including the perception of these words) is an external, physical world independent of us. Metaphysics makes room for the notion that what we call objects are primarily perceptions, only subsequently interpreted as coagulated objects. Notably, metaphysics can also take an opposing view. It can suggest there indeed is an external, physical world independent of us. The point is, both viewpoints are recognized as possible interpretations of what is happening before our eyes.

Increasingly, scientists are considering the former metaphysical view. They are exploring the possibility that the world we experience may be akin to a hallucination, and the universe may be a mental phenomenon rather than a physical thing. But there's a greater point here: What we call science has always been a process within metaphysics.

Once we make the metaphysical assumption that I, as an inquirer, can objectively study a world that is external to me, we have laid a metaphysical foundation for what we call science. When we further build the processes of hypothesizing, observing, and experimenting with those observations upon that foundation, we have begun the process we call science. All this is a metaphysical process, called by a different name. While we generally say that science and metaphysics are two different fields, we find that science cannot be done without establishing a metaphysical foundation, even if the foundation is subsequently forgotten.

It just so happens that most of our society has been unwittingly caught up in the materialist metaphysical view that most scientists share. Many if not most scientists themselves do not realize that they are operating in the field of metaphysics, having unwittingly absorbed a particular metaphysical platform from those they looked up to. The success of science has made it easy to ignore its origins. Ironically, it is that very success that is bringing science home to appreciate its roots once more. Neuroscience and physics in particular are leading the charge in reuniting the child with its parent.

Scientists are metaphysicians. In fact, we all are. It's time we recognize it. As we do, we will give ourselves permission to explore previously unrecognized regions of the mind, and our understanding of ourselves, the world, and science will evolve.

Chapter 17

The Myth of the Monkey Mind

The "monkey mind" is the term for the personal chatter that seemingly goes on inside our heads. On one hand, it can be helpful to label this chatter and begin a practice to help quiet it. But once we get to a point where the mind is relatively quiet, it's important to let go of the story of the monkey mind.

Holding on to the idea of the monkey mind reinforces the misunderstanding that the mind is "mine" or "me" or personal. The truth is the whole mind is decidedly not monkey-like. It seems monkey-like because we are paying attention to only a small fraction of it—our personal thoughts and feelings.

The mental chatter that we may subjectively experience is only a minute fraction of the mind. The key to seeing through the myth of the monkey mind is to recognize the rest of the mind—not just personal experiences, but all experiences.

Any and all experiences you have are the mind. Objects themselves are experiences of the mind, like gusts of wind in the open sky.

That means this screen or page is mind. These words are mind. The floor beneath you is mind. Even the sense of "you" as a localized experience in or near the body is mind. Consider how similar this is to a dream.

Notice these words, and consider that the feeling that it is "outside" of you is just another appearance. Notice the objects in the room... mind. Notice any confusion, tightness, resistance... also mind. Some of this mind is personal (your body, your personality), and some isn't.

As you begin to see this, habitual mental chatter will abate, because the mind is no longer being squeezed into a conceptual box we call the brain. It is allowed to be itself. The myth of the monkey mind evaporates.

Q&A

1. *When I try to meditate, my mind sure acts like a monkey.*

Yes, a *part* of the mind acts like a monkey. Before you meditate next time, look around you with your eyes open. Consider that everything you are experiencing, even with your eyes open, is the mind. After a while, let your eyes fall closed. It's likely that the monkey will be less active.

Chapter 18

What Is Consciousness?

Consciousness has always been a topic of interest to meditators. More recently, consciousness has increasingly become the focus of scientists worldwide. Attendance at conferences exploring consciousness is increasing. Robust, testable, scientific theories about consciousness are being proposed. Yet, while theories that attempt to measure consciousness are taking a step in the right direction, what they are measuring is not consciousness itself but rather the complexity of the mind.

The time is ripe for science to differentiate consciousness from mind.

So, what is consciousness? Let us start to answer this question by first examining the relationship between perception and the mind.

According to the theory of visual perception, you see a physical object like this screen because photons ricochet off the screen, strike your retina, and send an electrochemical impulse to your brain. There, in the dark, damp, mushy brain, a three-dimensional world bathed in light is created according to the nature of the impulse.

But where is the light that the brain supposedly creates? According to our theory, the light of the luminous sun at high noon is created in the brain. No anatomist has found light approaching such intensity in a neuron.

A further problem in the current theory of perception is that the brain itself is an object of perception not fundamentally different from other objects. If these words you are reading are a projection, then the brain is a projection as well. What is projecting the brain? Our theories of perception are useful, yet incomplete.

Enter mind, stage left. While mind is traditionally thought of as our subjective thoughts and feelings, in fact it is much more. It is the set of all experiences. This includes the experience of thought, emotion, memory, intuition, desire, identity, relationship, sensation, and perception, including the experience of perceiving so-called "physical" things. It includes the experience of individuality, separateness, space, and time. All experiences, gross and subtle, are the mind.

The brain is mental. The world is mental.

If everything we experience is the mind, including our own sense of identity, what could possibly be left? What could consciousness be?

Let's zoom in on the mind a bit more. Every experience of the mind has three parts: an experiencer, an experienced object, and the relationship between the two, which we call experiencing. For example, when I eat spaghetti, I am the experiencer, the spaghetti is the object of my experience, and tasting or eating it is the relationship between the two. This triadic nature of experience is ubiquitous for all experiences. Even in meditation, there is a meditator, the object of meditation (which may be as subtle as a thought or even silence), and there is the relationship between the two, which is attention.

There is only one experience which is not triadic: unitary experience. In unitary experience, the experiencer and the experienced object are integrated. (To be precise, the very word unity implies the possibility of duality and the triadic nature of experience, but we'll set that aside here for the purpose of understanding and come back to it in Part III.) They are not separate, and hence any sense of separation and limitation is absent. This unitary experience is consciousness. Another way to say this is that consciousness is not an experience in the traditional sense.

Naturally, consciousness is not a personal identity. It is not my consciousness or your consciousness. The levels and types of consciousness that science talks about (like your mind and my mind) are better described as levels of mind. Because science has not identified the deeper, unbounded consciousness that we are describing here, it uses the word in a different sense.

Consciousness has no parts, no distinguishing features within itself, just as water doesn't distinguish among ocean, wave, puddle, or ripple.

Ocean, wave, and ripple have unique characteristics, varying from large to small, but water does not recognize them as separate or different from itself as there is nothing in those entities that is different from water in the slightest.

Similarly, consciousness is seamless, seemingly a world apart from ever-changing experiences, yet the very substratum of the world.

Water itself seems to exist at a different level of reality from the ripple. But if water is removed from the ripple, not an iota of ripple can exist. Yet, if the activity of the ripple is removed from water, water is still water. Water is independent of the ripple, yet the ripple is entirely dependent on water. Similarly, consciousness is independent of mind and world, yet mind and world are entirely dependent on consciousness.

If you ask an insightful ripple that meditates regularly who she is, she will say, "I am an activity (or form, or part) of water," and she will be right from the standpoint of a subtle mind. If you ask water about the ripple, water would say, "What's a ripple? I alone am."

If we say that the ripple is the activity of water, we are not doing justice to water's perspective. On the other hand, if we say there is only water and there is no ripple, we are not doing justice to the ripple's perspective (or to her friends: ocean, wave, puddle, raindrop, etc.). The statement that best acknowledges the ripple's experience while also pointing out the next stage in the ripple's evolution is, "The ripple is the apparent activity of water."

Similarly, mind is the apparent activity of consciousness.

That statement is actually a pointer. If the ripple understands the pointer, it knows itself to be an activity. It knows that its own separate identity is dependent on its activity. If activity stops, the separate identity of the ripple stops, and any self-imposed difference from water will disappear. And slowly the insightful ripple becomes more still, until activity ceases, and the separate ripple sees through its boundary. When the boundary dissolves, it is seen that the ripple was indeed an appearance all along, with no independent existence apart from water. Once this is seen, the apparent activity of the ripple can reemerge, along with that of the wave, river, waterfall, etc., yet the knowledge that water alone exists shines through these appearances.

Similarly, mind is the apparent activity of consciousness. From the perspective of consciousness, there is no mind, no fluctuation, no activity. Consciousness is dimensionless, boundless, and seamless. It is infinity. From the perspective of the subtle mind, there is activity, there is fluctuation. To still the subtle mind, the pointer "mind is the apparent activity of consciousness" is given. The subtle mind then relaxes and relinquishes activity, and as a result merges into consciousness. The mind can then reemerge without forgetting that it is the apparent activity of consciousness, because it doesn't see itself as a separate entity any longer.

Consciousness is the heart of reality. It cannot be objectified by science, although science can and will reach the outer limits of the mind. The physical world is a subset of that mind, and you and I are individuated aspects of that mind. This is testable in the laboratory of your own experience. The answer to "What is consciousness?" resides within and beyond each one of us.

Chapter 19

What's the Purpose of All This?

A few months ago, I was speaking with a group of people about the relationship between consciousness, mind, and world. Someone stood up at the tail end of the conversation and asked a couple of core questions.

Why does consciousness appear as mind, which we then take to be physical things?

What's the purpose of all this?

This is a tricky question, and it has been answered from many perspectives. The spiritual answer is that this world is here for our evolution. Every experience we have is an opportunity to see the currents underlying our interpretation of what is happening. The scientific answer may be that this world is a random, purposeless occurrence, the freak outcome of the movement of cosmic ripples resulting from the Big Bang. The religious answer is that our purpose is to know and serve God.

But there is another possibility. The world may be a perceived reflection of what we are. When I take myself to be an individual, I perceive the world as a collection of individual, separate things. When I take myself as something subtler, then the world too appears subtler. And when I shed the layers of my costume to stand naked before the universe, then consciousness alone exists, with no separate universe projected within it.

The very question "What is the purpose of this universe?" is asked from the perspective of an individual identity, a character within the drama. Imagine if a character in your dream last night asked the same question to another dream-character. Nobody in the dream would really have a final answer, although all answers I first listed could be satisfying depending on the nature of the dream-character's mind. A more complete answer might be arrived at by asking, "What universe are you referring to, and how is it perceived?" This approach questions the very assumption of an independently existing universe.

The question of *why* the world exists is answered at the level of mind that asks the question. By questioning the very assumptions behind the question, a more complete answer can be discovered.

Q&A

1. *Are you saying that there is no universe, and therefore no purpose for life?*

No, I'm saying that consciousness alone exists and is interpreted as a universe. What we call "the universe" is nothing but consciousness, but that doesn't negate our interpretations of the universe. It's not about the words, it's about the recognition of what is independently real and what is interpretation. For example, at the relative level I'm a family member, citizen, physician, and so on. I do my best in each of these roles, and each has a purpose. That doesn't contradict the underlying awareness of the big picture.

2. *What about an overarching purpose beyond any one role? Is there an overall purpose for life?*

That would depend on the nature of the mind asking the question. If you ask me, a purpose could very well be for the individual to learn, grow, and discover more of oneself. However, that again would be with respect to the individual mind and not the complete picture. Purpose is relative to identity, just as everything is relative to identity.

Part III

The Many Masks of Non-Duality

Chapter 20

What Is Non-Duality?

In the last chapter, we distinguished between triadic experience and unitary experience. In triadic experience, there is a recognition of a sense of personal identity (no matter how contracted or expanded) and a recognition of some object that we are experiencing (no matter how gross or subtle). The relationship between the two forms the third part of the triadic experience.

We could simplify this categorization of triadic experiences by simply focusing on the two poles of each experience, namely the subject having the experience and the object being experienced. So, when I eat spaghetti, the personal sense of me is the subject and the spaghetti is the object. When I enjoy the warmth of sunshine on my face, the sense of me is again the subject and the warmth of the sunshine is the object. This apparent duality of me and not-me is what non-duality falsifies.

Once the personal, localized identity of *me* is assumed, an endless stream of sub-dualities spring forth from that perspective:

- I am *here* but I really need to get *there* (duality of space).
- *This* works better than *that* (duality of proximity).
- That happened *last* time but it won't happen *next* time (duality of sequence, or time).
- I'm feeling cold (as opposed to hot).
- The air conditioning is working (as opposed to not working).
- Our team won (as opposed to lost).

Of all these dualities, the starkest is the duality of the experiencer (subject) and the experienced (object). Cold and hot are opposites, but they're both experiences I'm having. The same is the case for winning and losing. Even more diametrically opposed than these are me, the subject, and whatever object it is I am experiencing.

Consciousness is the integration or healing of subject-object splitting. It is the whole that appears to split into subject and object. In the case of feeling the sunshine on my face, the sense of me as a separate identity and the sensation of warmth are both experienced as apparent modifications of what we call consciousness. Existing prior to the duality of subject and object, this consciousness is non-dual. It is absolutely homogenous, devoid of any kind of differentiation or perturbation, and prior to space and time (and therefore prior to perception and the objects of perception).

It is in reference to this consciousness, not my or your consciousness, that we speak of non-duality. It is this consciousness, the non-dual, which apparently differentiates into the familiar universe of space and time, along with its many perceivers and objects of perception. It is non-dual because it is beyond multiplicity, beyond duality, and beyond even oneness (more on this in the next chapter). Most importantly, the non-dual is your very nature beyond the personal sense of individuality and the expanded sense of oneness. It is not a concept, though the words used to describe it may begin as concepts. The non-dual is the You beyond you.

Chapter 21

How Is Non-Duality Different from Oneness?

We saw earlier that the strictly materialist mind primarily interprets a world of multiplicity, in which the individual perceives the many separate, independent, external objects of the world. The idealist mind, on the other hand, interprets primarily the singular mind, differentiating itself as objects in relation to personal, individuated minds.

One-ness describes the idealist mind. In the state of oneness, the connectivity between apparently separate things is experienced. The mind travels the full spectrum from separateness to connectedness, just as the violinist's bow sweeps across the strings from one end to the other. The feeling is one of expansion, because the individual is no longer limited to individuated and private sensory experience.

Yet both of these experiences, materialism and idealism, are in the world of space and time. Materialism positions itself within the interpreted physical dimension of space and time while idealism exists as the metaphysical space-time construct itself. The understanding and experience of space and time is different in each, but both are ultimately modifications of some underlying nature. In other words, as long as we are talking about forms and functions of any kind—physical, mental, or even subtler—we are still in the world of interpretation, whether gross or subtle.

The question remains: What is it that appears as forms and functions? What is it that appears as both the idealist and materialist mind? This is the question non-duality answers. What non-duality refers to as consciousness is beyond any kind of differentiation whatsoever.

It bears mentioning that differences in terminology are context-dependent. The word "oneness" is often used to explain non-dual philosophy, as I have done in an earlier chapter. Although the inquiring mind must start by clarifying such conceptual contradictions, they will continue to be bothersome so long as we insist on remaining at the level of concepts. We must clarify concepts until there is enough clarity to leap beyond the concept and recognize the truth behind it.

It's something like riding a bike. I can learn all about brakes, pedals, momentum, and balance, but at some point, all that must be left behind to simply ride, free of thought-interpretation. Similarly, once the true meaning of words like mind, consciousness, and non-duality are recognized, the words themselves become used shells. All philosophies are but vehicles.

Q&A

1. *I thought spiritual awakening was about oneness. Non-duality sounds confusing.*

Oneness is a dynamic experience. It is one end of a spectrum that ranges from separateness to connectedness to oneness. These are all states of the mind, with oneness being the most expansive and subtlest. Non-duality suggests this entire range, including oneness, is the dance of consciousness.

2. *So, as the mind becomes subtler, it approaches non-duality?*

As the mind becomes subtler, it approaches oneness. It becomes clear and recognizes that the one and the many play off each other—that oneness and multiplicity are two sides of the same coin. That recognition suggests that non-duality may be noticed—the coin itself may be noticed rather than the sides of the coin.

Chapter 22

Why Is the Non-Dual Referred to As Consciousness?

The term consciousness, as it is used in the context of non-dual philosophy, means something different than it does in other contexts, such as in neuroscience and in popular culture. In the previous chapter, I wrote that experiences can generally be described as either triadic or dualistic. This means that each experience is comprised of both a subject (the experiencer) and the object (the object being experienced). In neuroscience, the subject is a scientist, and the object might be a brain, neurons, or a pattern of behavior.

The limitation of the subject-object orientation is that from that viewpoint, we are unable to look behind the curtain and see what the common origin of both the scientist and the brain she is studying might be. We are not asking what the origin of the scientist is, and further, we are mistakenly assuming that an answer to that question would not significantly bear on our understanding of the object being studied. We are beginning the study of the object after assuming the separate and independent reality of the scientist. Of course, great pains are taken to minimize the bias of the scientist in any experiment, but none of these great pains can come to bear on the point that the observing scientist and the object of observation are fundamentally not different, though they are perceived differently.

If the same non-duality is prior to both the scientist and the brain she is studying, then the non-dual is also not physical, because at the level of physicality the scientist and object of study appear different. Furthermore, if the non-dual is not physical, it is not restricted by the confines of space and time. Remember that by the non-dual, I'm not referring to the smaller, localized parts of the scientist and the brain, like molecules or atoms. I'm referring to that which underlies all materiality itself. From that perspective, the physical world goes from being independent objects to a world of mind, and ultimately to a world that is beyond all form and function. That world (this very world, in fact) is referred to as consciousness.

But why is it called *consciousness*?

This word *consciousness* as it is used in non-dual philosophy serves as a placeholder, much like the variable X is a placeholder in algebra. Until I can solve for X and know what it represents, I need the symbol X to make sense of the relationships between the other characters in the equation. Similarly, until I know what the word *consciousness* actually represents beyond the common use of the word, I can use it as a symbol to recognize the relationships between all other experiences I have, such as world, mind, subjective, objective, mental, physical, and so on.

So why use the word *consciousness* at all? Why not come up with some new word? In the Indian non-dual philosophical tradition of Advaita Vedanta, that "new" word is Brahman, which roughly translates to "the big." (It is a very specific word in that it turns an adjective (big) into a noun (the big), which has important implications that we won't enter into here. Suffice it to say that Brahman is neither big in the adjectival sense nor small.)

Another more descriptive Sanskrit word for consciousness is *satchitananda*, which translates to existence-consciousness-limitlessness or existence-knowledge-bliss, depending on the translation. This tripartite descriptive word is a symbol of something that is partition-less. The limits of cumbersome language, which can only describe finite aspects of the mind, are evident here.

The word *consciousness* is used in non-dual philosophy as a simpler synonym of the other words just mentioned. Therefore, we must be careful not to confuse this use of the word consciousness with the more common, popular use, which is that of an individual's personal consciousness, or mind. There are many minds, but there are not many consciousness-es. There is no plural form of consciousness in non-duality. In the most precise sense, neither does consciousness represent the singular. Rather it is non-dual, beyond both multiplicity and oneness.

By using the word *consciousness* as a symbol (just as we use ∞ as a symbol of the non-finite), we know that it is somehow intimately connected to us. After all, if you are conscious, then whatever is called consciousness must somehow be connected to you. Therefore, whatever it is that is underlying this interpreted world, whether from the materialist or idealist perspective, must be knowable in some way.

This usage of consciousness as ultimate reality may also go by other names, including pure consciousness, universal consciousness, universal mind, awareness, and being. Mathematics calls it infinity. Philosophy calls it reality or truth. Religion may call it God with a capital G. Different minds use words differently.

Despite the confusing connotations associated with the word *consciousness*, I rather like the word to represent the non-dual because it brings up the latent confusions and apparent contradictions that exist. Depending on the background of each person, words such as consciousness, mind, world, identity, and experience can have different meanings. It's helpful to bring these differences to the surface and address them directly so we can understand each other better.

Ultimately, non-dual philosophy is not about language or concepts, which are stepping stones for the inquiring mind. Having recognized what the philosophy is trying to communicate, the mind no longer clings to the particular meaning of a word. Thereafter, particular words are used solely for the purpose of consistency in communication.

Chapter 23

Why Does Non-Duality Contradict Itself?

Whenever non-duality is presented in words, as it is through speaking and writing, it is filtered through the mind. The words on this page represent my mind and my assumptions, which are specific to the experiences I've accumulated over the years. So, while there are no differences in non-duality, there are myriad ways of trying to communicate it, as there are for any topic.

In addition, differences in messaging account for the varying natures of the minds receiving the message. Which assumptions about the world and the sense of personal identity will be accepted by a particular audience? Which will be rejected? Which are up for consideration? Depending on the mind of the audience, the language must change.

For example, as I've written these chapters, I've generally acknowledged that we as human beings have a sense of individual identity, we have a body, we have a personal mind of thoughts and emotions, and that there seems to be some sense of separation between us and the world. I also often bring in the themes of science and philosophy to show that science, philosophy, and self-inquiry operate along different ranges of the mind.

But I've also written that experiences—including the experience of a body, a localized sense of personal identity, and of physical objects in the world—are mental in nature. I lump these various kinds of experience together to focus on what is common to them all—mind. That will be effective for some people, but not for others.

Other people communicate non-duality differently. Some will go into detail about many aspects of the human psyche—emotions, thoughts, desires, intuition, memory, and so on. Each of these can be discussed at length, which can be quite helpful for some.

Some people will spend more time focusing on repressed emotions and thoughts, which can keep the mind bogged down and unable to see clearly. Specific techniques can be taught by which these "blockages" can be released to see more clearly.

Some will deny the existence of cause and effect. They would disagree with the previous paragraph, which suggested that we can do something to clarify the mind, or even that we need to.

Others will deny that "you" exist at all. They might suggest that the sense of "me" and "you" isn't real and doesn't exist to begin with, and therefore that non-duality already is the case. In other words, we shouldn't bother trying.

Some will avoid using the word "I" in trying to communicate non-duality. They will linguistically represent the impersonal sense of individuality (or non-individuality) by referring to themselves in the third person, or perhaps not at all.

Some say there's only one thing to be done: See right through this experience. It's all here in and beyond this experience if one can see right through it.

Some won't tell any stories. They won't talk about non-duality because, well, there's nothing to talk about it seems.

Finally, even these descriptions I've just provided make a few assumptions, which themselves can be questioned.

None of these perspectives are new. All of them have been around for millennia. Some stories complement the others while some contradict the others. This is because the sense of personhood or identity to which these stories are addressed is different in each case. The important question is: Which story questions your assumptions?

Different strokes for different folks. Pick the one that resonates with you. Or simply walk on.

Chapter 24

Are There Degrees of Non-Duality?

The prior chapter provides important context for this chapter. Please keep it in mind as you read on.

There are no degrees of non-duality. There are no different depths, no progression, no deepening, nothing of the sort. This is why non-duality seems radical.

On the other hand, there are degrees of mind. The mind can range from gross to subtle, from misunderstanding to understanding, from confusion to clarity. The mind can evolve from materialism to panpsychism to idealism.

Non-duality is beyond these states of mind, yet its expression through the mind becomes clearer as the mind becomes clearer. Non-duality is equally neither materialism nor idealism, yet when we speak about non-duality it has to be spoken about in terms of the world and in terms of concepts. This is why, in the Indian philosophy of Advaita Vedanta, various threads of non-dual philosophy are delivered, each beginning at the level of the inquirer's mind. Some begin with questioning materialism, others begin with questioning idealism, and yet others begin somewhere in between. All ultimately converge in questioning any notion of difference, no matter how subtle, yielding the realization that consciousness alone is. Here, even the word *alone* is a compromise, reflecting a mind that still entertains the possibility of duality.

In Indian philosophy, there are different interpretations of non-duality. For example, there is qualified non-duality, which says that the non-dual alone exists, but is qualified by multiplicity. This is awfully similar to idealism, which says mind alone exists and appears as a world of multiplicity, including matter.

From the perspective of unqualified non-duality, however, such concepts don't exist. Non-duality unabashedly says that consciousness alone is. Nothing further is said unless there is confusion about this statement. Common misinterpretations of this statement include:

- The whole world is in my head.
- I can do whatever I want because this world is only a dream.
- Non-duality is a way to escape from the world.
- Everything is conscious in a personal sense.

Usually, the inquiring mind demands an explanation beyond "Consciousness alone is" because the mind has already interpreted the world, whether as mind (idealism), matter (materialism), or some combination of the two (panpsychism). While such explanations of the world are readily given, non-dual philosophy simultaneously says that they are false in the ultimate sense. They are rungs in the ladder of insight that are distinct from non-duality itself.

What makes non-dual philosophy distinct is that not only does it say that the physical world is the dance of the mind, but it also says that the very perception of difference is an appearance of an underlying reality. At the level of that reality, there are no differences.

Chapter 25

On Science, Spirituality, and Consciousness

It is important to distinguish non-duality itself from the philosophy of non-duality. Philosophy is a process of thinking that appears in the non-dual. Similarly, science is a process of observing, hypothesizing, and experimenting that appears in the non-dual.

Today, there is much talk about the overlap between science and spirituality. Some say this talk of overlap is premature and confuses both fields, but I disagree. Although the overlap has not been completely fleshed out, its exploration is right on course.

Discoveries in physics over the last century suggest that what we call a physical thing, like this laptop I'm typing on, may fundamentally not be physical. (This again leads to the familiar question: What does the word *physical* mean?) When we zoom in closely enough, the particularity that seems to make up this laptop starts to disappear. Thinking along these lines and following the evidence led physicist Richard Conn Henry to the idealist conclusion, "The Universe is entirely mental," and, "The Universe is immaterial..." ("The Mental Universe," *Nature*, July 2005).

He is not alone in his scientific views. Many other pioneering physicists came to similar conclusions long ago, including Max Planck, one of the originators of quantum theory, who famously said, "I regard consciousness as fundamental. I regard matter as derivative from consciousness." Importantly, he is using the word *consciousness* in a way that is consistent with non-dual philosophy.

Consciousness is the fundamental factor that gives birth to both science and spirituality. In this sense, science and spirituality are not fundamentally different. Both are local, personal activities of a greater non-local mind experiencing itself through different lenses. Science begins less subjectively (with a focus on the personal experience of inter-subjective agreement) and spirituality begins more subjectively (with a focus on the very notion of a personal experience).

Science is currently mired in materialist philosophy, but we are already seeing a movement from materialism to panpsychism to even idealism. At each stop along the way, the primacy of matter is further questioned and seen through, and mind takes a more prominent role. Science is getting there via quantum physics, which is a gateway to contemplating and questioning the apparent duality of mind and matter.

On the other hand, the spiritual aspirant begins with the mind—usually the personal mind, not mind-as-universe. Through introspection and meditation, the aspirant comes to recognize the mind-as-universe (idealism). Matter is contextualized in mind.

Science and spirituality travel apparently divergent paths, loop around, and ultimately discover the limitations of splitting the world into subjective and objective perspectives. The reconciliation of subject and object into non-duality goes by many names, but ultimately it is neither scientific nor spiritual. All dualities must be left behind.

Science and spirituality are a few good conversations and insights away from being on the same page. How long that takes is up to us.

Chapter 26

Can Science Be Derived from Non-Duality?

Yes. Both science and spirituality can be derived from non-duality. The key step in the derivation is examining what a boundary is.

A boundary is what makes a thing distinct. For example, the boundary around this page is what makes this page distinct from the surrounding space. The boundary around your body is what makes it distinct. Similarly, a boundary is what makes a particle, a particle. It's what makes a number, a number.

So, what is a boundary, after all?

Science and spirituality will take different approaches to this question. Science examines the boundary around apparently external and physical objects, while spirituality examines the personal sense of identity that makes the individual feel separate and different from the surrounding world.

Both approaches will ultimately agree on one idea: All boundaries require space to exist. If there is no space, no boundary can be drawn. So, let's take a closer look at space.

If I measure the gap between two pieces of furniture and note that the gap is one meter long, I might say that a meter of space separates the two items. If I take a rocket to the moon, I might say that I covered about a quarter of a million miles of space on my journey. In both cases, we are defining space as an interval between two points. One point cannot define space. Two points are required.

If I go to sleep at night and take a rocket to the moon in my dream, my team of fellow dream-scientists would calculate that I traveled a quarter of a million miles of space. Yet is there any actual space in the dream? Did my dream-character actually travel that many miles? Was the size of my dream stretched out to a quarter of a million miles? Of course not. From the perspective of a shift in consciousness (which is what we call waking up in the morning), those quarter of a million miles are known to surely be a projection, along with the projection of an individual *me* in the dream, a dream-rocket, and a dream-moon.

This is the first hint to understanding space: What is recognized as space in one state of consciousness is recognized as a projection of the mind in another state of consciousness. But that still doesn't explain why I perceive the space that separates me here on Earth from the moon up there in the sky. What is it about non-dual consciousness or my mind that creates the perception of space? Another way to ask this question is: What are the two points that define the perception of space in day-to-day experience? Those two points are two of the most common words we use: *here* and *there*.

Here is what I call a place where I feel that my identity has localized. For example, wherever my body is standing is called *here*. Wherever it is not standing is called *there*. Think about it— wherever you are (meaning wherever your sense of identity is localized) is always called *here*. It doesn't matter if you're awake, dreaming, on the moon, or underwater. Wherever you perceive your identity to be is *here*. And every other place is called *there*. This interval between *here* and *there* is what the mind interprets as space. Therefore, without the metaphysical localization of identity that we call *here*, the first point that makes the interval of space possible cannot exist. No localization of identity = no space.

While I'm in the dream and believe I'm the dream-character, space appears to be real. It would seem preposterous for the dream-character to suggest to other dream-characters that, "Space is a projection and not independently real," because all the other characters would also have established the here-there or me-not me axis on which space depends. However, on waking up from the dream, the me-not me illusion evaporates, and along with it, the interpretation of space. Space is metaphysical, not physical.

Once the metaphysical space defined by *here* has localized, all *theres* become possible. The space between the Earth and the moon is the measured interval between two *theres*, namely a point *there* on Earth (such as Cape Canaveral in Florida, USA) and a point *there* on the moon (such as the Alpine Valley). If the witness is a localized "form-al" (having form) identity, the observed world appears as having fixed forms. If the witness is delocalized, or non-local, the world appears as potential forms. Thus, we can say the world exists both as potential and as form (and everything in between), depending on the condition of the observer, or witness. There is an intrinsic formless/form complementarity to this world.

If we want to measure one such form, we have to form-alize space by switching into a localized, fixed identity-state, thereby engaging the world as a fixed, physical projection. The very fact that we do this means the world is not independent of us.

The potential world has no need for physical space or time, just as the dream has no need for an independently real space or time. Trillions upon trillions of miles can appear and innumerable eons can come and go in the mind without any independent need for a millimeter of space or a millisecond of time.

Localization of identity and the concomitant projection of space and its embedded objects are the natural tendencies of the personal mind. It happens in the dream state and in this waking state. The mechanics of dream state and waking state projections (like the one you're experiencing now) are the same. This is why physical objects seem to disappear on close scientific investigation of their component parts—they aren't independently real and they aren't independently physical. They are entirely space-dependent, and therefore, mind-dependent.

But surely space can't only be a projection! Objects still exist in space even if you're not looking at them, don't they? You're not saying that if you're not looking at the sun, the sun disappears, are you?!

The question is—disappears *as what* and *to whom*? If I'm not looking at the sun, then yes, it disappears to me as a localized witness, obviously. If you are looking at the sun, then it doesn't disappear to you. On the other hand, the sun we interpret may not be interpreted the same way by another species with another nervous system, therefore it would disappear as the sun you and I know and love, and would appear in a different way to another species. If *nobody* is looking at the sun, then the question doesn't make any sense. The sun that we speak of is indeterminate, in a potential state.

Appearances and disappearances are always relative to an observer, or witness. No witness = no appearance *as that particular form*. (The formless/form complementarity rises again.) This doesn't mean that the intrinsic existence of the object is gone. The "object" can still exist as potential, or, to make it more easily digestible, as information or energy, but as a formed object it only has existence relative to an observer with a particular nervous system that interprets that particular form.

The implication is that there is no independently objective world. All we can say with intellectual rigor is that we, as observers sharing the same type of nervous system, can claim inter-subjective agreement about the existence of an apparently external object like the sun.

Thus, a few key insights to reconciling space and non-duality are:

1. Space is the interval between two points.
2. The first two points that define the interval of space are created by the sense of localized identity (here) and the sense of non-identity elsewhere (there).
3. Space is metaphysical. What is recognized as space in one state of consciousness (localized identity) is recognized as

a projection of the mind in another state of consciousness (delocalized identity).

4. Once the first metaphysical point that defines space (here) is localized, the world appears to localize and be full of separate, independent, physical objects. This is "physical" space.

5. Where there is no localization of identity, space cannot exist.

Epilogue

I remember being at the back of the classroom in my ninth-grade math class while Mr. Black was scribbling on the chalkboard. I remember wondering when he was going to get to the really interesting part—the part about how mathematics could be used to represent how human beings experience the world. It never came.

I remember dissection lab in Mrs. Schlossnagle's eleventh grade class. I thought it would give me answers to the questions I had about the body and what it was made of. It didn't.

I remember the tremendous volume of information I learned in medical school and residency training. It answered many questions, but still left one unanswered: *What is the nature of the human being?*

Many would say that our school systems are not meant to answer such questions. Those questions are only supposed to be answered on Sundays, or by parents or "spiritual people." Or maybe in a graduate level course. Yet, our schools do answer them—unintentionally, by *not* addressing them and instead focusing on everything else. The message they send is that everything around you is important and everything you might achieve is important, but the *you* at the center of it all is a topic that's off limits. Children that grow up in such an educational system learn to divert their attention from their intuitive understanding of themselves and the world to external matters that adults are telling them are more important. They create a schism in their experience of the world—the shell of *what I should be* becomes more important than the core of *what I am*.

This is slowly changing. More schools are including an exploration of emotions, thoughts, and the mind in their curriculum, an approach that demands the teacher is also actively engaged in self-exploration. It's a good start.

An exploration of *what I am* does not have to be overly intellectualized or complicated. Children have a feel for it already. All we need to do is not distract them from that as they learn new information. They can learn everything in the existing curriculum within the greater context of a growing appreciation of who and what they are. This is the highest form of learning. School is not the only place one can receive this education, but it surely should be one of them.

If a child grows up devoid of this context, they will tend to see the world as separate and different from themselves. They will tend to forget that what they essentially are is not different from what the world essentially is. They will tend to create a divide between so-called "worldly knowledge" and "spiritual knowledge." There are no two such categories. Knowledge is knowledge. We are the ones who superimpose the divisions of the mind on it.

A divided mind can still go on to achieve great successes in life, but they will be limited. No matter how great the outer accolades, there will still be a sense that something is missing below the surface until the divisions are reconciled. That division will also be reflected in the work they produce as adults and in the society we see around us.

As it stands now, we implicitly teach a materialist philosophy to our children starting in elementary school simply because that is how most adults perceive the world—as a separate, external, independent thing. We are doing it without explicitly saying a word about it. It's conveyed in our thoughts, our actions, and the way we interact with others.

The onus is on us to recognize this. Our youngest children see the world differently than we do, and it's not because they don't know enough about the world. It's because we haven't put what we know in context.

We could argue here about which philosophy is right and which is wrong, but ultimately this isn't about philosophy.

Philosophy is a tool for the mind—a way to put a frame around what's happening. It is not the goal. That's why this book is meant for reflection, not convincing. A person can't be convinced of something that contradicts their sense of identity. But anyone can appreciate that the sense of who or what we are is key to how we relate to the world. We can start from that common understanding.

I've written about children in this conclusion because these were the experiences I had as a child growing up and attending school. I think we can do better. That starts with you and me. This is about our experience of life, now. It's about what's happening on center stage, now. It's about seeing right through the philosophies, practices, authority figures, and ultimately, the sense of identity, now. It's about seeing what has always been and what always will be.

Timeless, infinite, pristine. This is You.

Author Biography

Anoop Kumar, MD, MM is a board-certified emergency physician practicing in the Washington, DC area. He also holds a master's degree in Management with a focus in Health Leadership. As a child, Anoop was exposed to the ancient Indian philosophy of Advaita Vedanta, better known as Non-Duality. He used the philosophy as a framework to experiment with his own experience of life. Today, he enjoys exploring and communicating about the intersection of consciousness and everything else.

Previous Books

Michelangelo's Medicine: How Redefining the Human
Body Will Transform Health and Healthcare
ISBN: 978-0997339604

Your body is much more than a collection of organs. It is a masterpiece, waiting to be discovered. Over the course of his career as an emergency physician, Dr. Anoop Kumar has come to recognize that what we have learned about the human body is remarkably incomplete and outdated. In these pages, he offers insights into:

- Why reconsidering what we've been told about our bodies is essential to healing and well-being.
- What the complete anatomy of a human being looks like.
- How a new framework for understanding the human body will help create a more inclusive and complete health care system.
- What you can do now to start experiencing well-being.

Personal and profound, these pages take us inside the mind of an emergency physician as he realizes that honoring his patients and his profession requires challenging the dogma of medical science and offering a unifying vision for well-being and health care.

Reviews
"You won't find this information in any medical school texts or lecture room, but therein lies the problem. As a physician myself, I often felt like something was amiss from my training, something hard to describe... This book offers hope that a new healthcare system that prioritizes wellness and well-being

alongside our current disease-care system will rejuvenate the malaise that I believe is troubling our current system. Dr. Kumar offers specific suggestions on how to get there."

"Dr. Kumar envisions the role of a true health care system; focusing not only on the disease but on complete well-being... Powerful, beautifully written, full of ideas and solutions!! Highly recommended!"

"Should be required reading! Whether you have been exposed to integrative medicine or are involved in conventional medicine practice, Dr. Kumar's *Michelangelo's Medicine* is an inspirational and compelling must-read for health, medical, nursing students and healers."

From the Author

Thank you for purchasing *Is This a Dream?* If you enjoyed this book and would like to connect further, please visit my website for news on upcoming events, courses, recent blog posts, and to sign up for my newsletter: http://www.anoopkumar.com.

If you'd like to further clarify the reflections in this book, check out the videos, courses, and other resources available on the website.

Sincerely,

Anoop

MANTRA
BOOKS

EASTERN RELIGION & PHILOSOPHY

We publish books on Eastern religions and philosophies. Books
that aim to inform and explore the various traditions that began in
the East and have migrated West.
If you have enjoyed this book, why not tell other readers by
posting a review on your preferred book site.

Recent bestsellers from MANTRA BOOKS are:

The Way Things Are
A Living Approach to Buddhism
Lama Ole Nydahl
An introduction to the teachings of the Buddha, and how to make use of these teachings in everyday life.
Paperback: 978-1-84694-042-2 ebook: 978-1-78099-845-9

Back to the Truth
5000 Years of Advaita
Dennis Waite
A demystifying guide to Advaita for both those new to, and those familiar with this ancient, non-dualist philosophy from India.
Paperback: 978-1-90504-761-1 ebook: 978-184694-624-0

Shinto: A celebration of Life
Aidan Rankin
Introducing a gentle but powerful spiritual pathway reconnecting humanity with Great Nature and affirming all aspects of life.
Paperback: 978-1-84694-438-3 ebook: 978-1-84694-738-4

In the Light of Meditation
Mike George
A comprehensive introduction to the practice of meditation and the spiritual principles behind it. A 10 lesson meditation programme with CD and internet support.
Paperback: 978-1-90381-661-5

A Path of Joy
Popping into Freedom
Paramananda Ishaya
A simple and joyful path to spiritual enlightenment.
Paperback: 978-1-78279-323-6 ebook: 978-1-78279-322-9

The Less Dust the More Trust
Participating in The Shamatha Project, Meditation and Science
Adeline van Waning, MD PhD
The inside-story of a woman participating in frontline meditation research, exploring the interfaces of mind-practice, science and psychology.
Paperback: 978-1-78099-948-7 ebook: 978-1-78279-657-2

I Know How To Live, I Know How To Die
The Teachings of Dadi Janki: A warm, radical, and life-affirming view of who we are, where we come from, and what time is calling us to do
Neville Hodgkinson
Life and death are explored in the context of frontier science and deep soul awareness.
Paperback: 978-1-78535-013-9 ebook: 978-1-78535-014-6

Living Jainism
An Ethical Science
Aidan Rankin, Kanti V. Mardia
A radical new perspective on science rooted in intuitive awareness and deductive reasoning.
Paperback: 978-1-78099-912-8 ebook: 978-1-78099-911-1

Ordinary Women, Extraordinary Wisdom
The Feminine Face of Awakening
Rita Marie Robinson
A collection of intimate conversations with female spiritual teachers who live like ordinary women, but are engaged with their true natures.
Paperback: 978-1-84694-068-2 ebook: 978-1-78099-908-1

The Way of Nothing
Nothing in the Way
Paramananda Ishaya
A fresh and light-hearted exploration of the amazing reality of
nothingness.
Paperback: 978-1-78279-307-6 ebook: 978-1-78099-840-4

Readers of ebooks can buy or view any of these bestsellers by
clicking on the live link in the title. Most titles are published in
paperback and as an ebook. Paperbacks are available in traditional
bookshops. Both print and ebook formats are available online.

Find more titles and sign up to our readers' newsletter at
http://www.johnhuntpublishing.com/mind-body-spirit.
Follow us on Facebook at https://www.facebook.com/OBooks
and Twitter at https://twitter.com/obooks.